This book should be returned to any branch of the
Lancashire County Library on or before the date

- 2 DEC 2016 ·		2/16.
2 9 DEC 2016		
2 0 FEB 2017 8/7/19.		
1 ᴜ OCT 2022		

ide

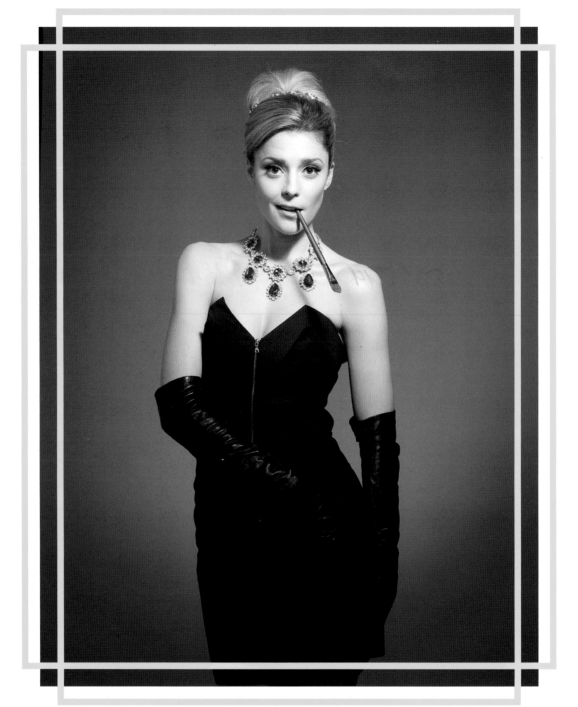

GRACE&STYLE

The Art of Pretending You Have It

Grace Helbig

SIMON &
SCHUSTER

London · New York · Sydney · Toronto · New Delhi

A CBS COMPANY

First published in Great Britain by Simon & Schuster UK Ltd, 2016
A CBS COMPANY

1 3 5 7 9 10 8 6 4 2

Simon & Schuster UK Ltd
1st Floor
222 Gray's Inn Road
London WC1X 8HB

www.simonandschuster.co.uk

Simon & Schuster Australia, Sydney
Simon & Schuster India, New Delhi

The author and publishers have made all reasonable efforts to contact copyright-holders for
permission, and apologise for any omissions or errors in the form of credits given. Corrections
may be made to future printings.

A CIP catalogue record for this book is available from the British Library

ISBN: 978-1-4711-5251-1
Ebook ISBN: 978-1-4711-5252-8

Interior design by Shawn Dahl, dahlimama inc
Photographs by Robin Roemer

Printed in Italy by L.E.G.O SpA

This book is dedicated to insecurity and fear.

Two of my best friends and closest enemies.

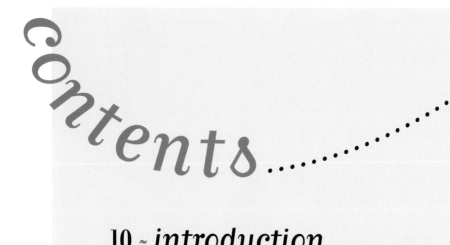

contents

grace & style

181 ~ life...style

introduction

My eating disorder started during my senior year of high school.

WHOA. I KNOW. WAY TO KICK THINGS OFF ON A FUN, LIGHTHEARTED NOTE, HELBIG.

But let's just go with it for a second. Because this book, this smattering of my thoughts on style and fashion and beauty, has been a really difficult thing for me to wrap my head around. I assumed it'd be easy to brain-barf some HILARIOUS feelings about tank tops and tube socks onto paper, but every time I tried to sit down to do it, I hit a wall. And then another wall. And another. Any countries out there looking to send a message to their neighbors and need help? Turns out I'm really great at putting up walls. НАНАНАНА, *depressing sigh*.

Once I started investigating why I was having so much trouble writing, I realized that no matter how funny you try to make the concept of beauty, it can still be a personal and sensitive topic for a lot of people, myself included. And I didn't want to pretend otherwise. And I *definitely* didn't want anything in this book to come across as arrogant or preachy because I've been negatively affected by the people and the images and the concepts touted by the fashion industries, so the last thing I want to do is trigger any insecurities you might have.

I wanted to take a second at the beginning of this book to give you a quick overview of my history of insecurity before getting into my present-day reflections on style. This is one part selfish and one part hopefully helpful. Selfish, because one of the ways I got out of the darkest period of my eating disorder was by talking about it; and hopefully helpful, because another way I got out of feeling so alone was by reading a butt-ton of books written by women who had also struggled with their body image. You see, YouTube didn't exist during that time; instead, I bought books hoping to hear someone else's story of suffering so I might feel less alone . . . BOOKS, YOU GUYS. So, who knows, my hope is that sharing this pretty sad personal time in my

Or maybe you're just here to find out five great tips for avoiding camel toe.

life might allow one singular person to feel less alone. And that's completely worth it.

Or maybe you're here to find out five great tips for avoiding camel toe. That's great, too! And trust me, we'll get to that!

I was a jock in high school. I was on the tennis team every fall, the indoor track team every winter, and the outdoor track team every spring. I grew up doing gymnastics and playing soccer and football with my brothers, so sports became my outlet. I also grew up socially awkward, so more individualized sports, like tennis and track, became my jam.

During the fall of my senior year of high school, I worked my way up to third singles on the tennis team (tennis teams have a hierarchy—you have to work your way up from playing doubles to playing singles—at least that's how it worked in Jersey, maybe that's completely wrong and when every other state decided how

high school tennis teams worked, Jersey was too busy buying test-tube shots and it missed the general consensus). Though I mostly played singles matches that season, depending on the team we went up against I occasionally played doubles with my friend Maddy, who was a grade below me.

Everyone on the team loved Maddy, myself included. She was fun and outgoing and pretty and incredibly silly. The idea of "consequences" never seemed to exist in her mental filing cabinets. Every away match we had, she'd try to moon at least one car driving behind our bus, even if it was our sixty-year-old coach at the wheel. She had a great sense of humor and an effortlessly charming chaos about her that I envied. Maddy and I were both lanky, sloppy tennis players, so it was always fun playing doubles with her. She'd scream nonsensical things whenever she missed a shot and we'd spend most of our matches laughing at our dumb mistakes. She never took it too seriously, which was the best because at the end of the day, it was *HIGH SCHOOL* tennis. She brought out a lot of the dumb, fun side of me that I wasn't confident enough to bring out on my own. I could never understand how she seemed so free of insecurities and fear.

On top of all of that, everyone on the team used to say we looked "exactly alike" and that we could be "twins." Which always made me feel good and slightly embarrassed because I thought Maddy was really pretty and I thought no one ever looked at me. Except one day someone casually tossed aside a comment that Maddy was "skinnier" than me.

Cue the record-player scratch.

Huh?

I knew it wasn't said with malicious intent, but it was something I just couldn't get myself to unhear. I had never really considered my body or its shape before. I had lean genes via my parents and I had always been active. I also didn't get my period until my senior year, so my boobs and hips were nowhere to be found. I was tall and lanky and uncomfortable; I was like a walking stick bug.

Still, I couldn't understand why skinniness was even a thing to remark on? Was it important? It must be important. Everyone loved Maddy. So if I want to be loved like Maddy, I should be more like Maddy. I should get *skinnier* (thank God for my high-school-level deductive-reasoning skills).

So that's what I did. That winter I started focusing on my fitness. I started working out on my own after my winter and spring track practices and spent my free time looking up and making healthy, low-calorie recipes from food websites. My antisocial self loved having something to focus on other than a constant fear of human interaction. But my newfound healthy hobby quickly became my secret, obsessive game.

During the summer of 2003, after I graduated high school and before I started college, I occasionally joined my high school's cross-country team on long-distance runs because my younger brother was on the team. One day one of my track coaches, who also coached this particular team, pulled me aside and asked me if I was okay. He thought I looked thin and was worried. I immediately felt weirded out and totally embarrassed. Someone was noticing me. Noticing my body. Noticing it change. I immediately deflected any of my coach's concerns. In my head I was only doing normal teenage girl things. I read workout magazines like everyone else, I watched runway fashion shows on the Style Network like everyone else, I ran on a treadmill while watching the Food Network LIKE everyone else. At that point I was limiting myself to twelve hundred calories a day and trying to exercise at least an hour a day because I had read that it was the ideal combo for losing weight. This was normal grown-up girl stuff, said all the glossy magazines with endless photos of fit ladies smiling while running in teeny-tiny workout shorts. Those ladies were clearly happy, and I was on my way to being happy, too. *My coach doesn't know what he's talking about*, I told myself. But secretly, after that interaction, I felt a sense of happiness that my weight loss had been acknowledged. It meant my plan was working. I was "winning" my game.

And with that twisted feeling, things got worse.

When I finally got to college, the combination of my social stiltedness and my oblivious ED went hand in hand. I kept myself from the painful awkwardness of socializing by focusing my free time on work and working out. Throughout my four years in college, I always had at least two jobs and spent upward of two hours a day in the gym. All while still restricting myself to a thousand to twelve hundred calories a day. Because I was alone so much, there was no one to tell me I was doing anything wrong. From my point of view, I was losing weight and gaining control. I hadn't reached "happiness" just yet, but I kept thinking I was getting closer.

The other way I occupied my time was by emailing sh*ttily cropped photos of myself to modeling agencies in NYC. I know, it's embarrassing even to type. I went to a small liberal-arts college in northern New Jersey about forty-five minutes outside of NYC. So, after watching hours of runway shows through high school and being five-nine and told more than a couple of times by randoms and family members that *You should be a model*, I sincerely thought I should try it. Finally, for who knows what reason, a tiny agency called Pretend Model Scouts (PMS for short) signed me. In hindsight, they were so small, there's a chance they were a drug front, but at the time it was a sign that my hard work was paying off. They sent me on "go-sees"* and casting calls and I was awful at all of it. But it turned out that the fashion industry itself was also pretty awful at it. I remember a man at Donald Trump's modeling agency telling me that one of my eyelids was fatter than the other and that it was a big concern for them. Beauty is measured in symmetry and clearly my right eyelid didn't get that memo. Did you know that eyelids could be fat? According to an unhappy forty-year-old man whose job it was to judge teenage bodies, they can! Clearly, I'm very over what he said.

I only booked two things in the year I was signed with PMS. One was a Tommy Hilfiger commercial with Christina Milian in which the director kept yelling at me to look less sad and scared, and where another model actually said to me with such pride during a lunch break that she hadn't eaten a full meal all day, only snacks. The other job was a respectably amateur runway show in a hotel lobby on the Upper East Side where I watched three European models who didn't speak English share six

*Go-see: a meeting/interview set up with an important designer or company that's supposed to help elevate your career.

Thin Mints. The year was a whirlwind of culture and education.

My time with modeling and with PMS faded away a few months later. Between school and work, it was harder to get into the city at a moment's notice for a casting. Also I hated it. And that was sort of important to consider in my decision-making process. It's also possible PMS's hypothetical drug fronting got busted and I just never found out and never had the desire or courage to follow up on it.

So I got back to my solo game bubble. The next couple years of college got pretty dark. I won't go into all the details because it still feels uncomfortable and kind of humiliating, but I'll give you some broad strokes.

All of my time outside of class and work (and all of my thoughts while in class and at work) became about working out and food. I got myself into a cycle of hiding and bingeing and purging. Never purging by vomiting, instead by intensely working out. Though I did try to make myself puke numerous times thinking it would be easier, but my body just couldn't do it—present-day Grace thanks you, body. Things got obsessive. The weirder my behavior got, the more private I became. And the more private I became, the weirder my behavior got. One summer I was working at an Applebee's in South Jersey and living at my dad's house. That summer I got into a daily pattern of not eating during my restaurant shifts, but instead bingeing afterward on bags of Chex Mix and spending two to three hours on my stepmom's elliptical at night after she and my dad fell asleep. And STILL I thought this behavior was TOTALLY normal. LOL. Cool job, self.

I was tired and repressed and sad all the time. I was losing weight and losing hair (surprise! That happens when your body loses too much weight! Fun discovery!). My relationships with friends and family were strained and superficial. I even had my first, real college boyfriend at the time, but we clearly weren't a good match.

He was preoccupied with himself and I was preoccupied with my ED. We were a match made in self-centered heaven.

Eventually he and I faded out and, by some weird miracle, I found myself in a new relationship with someone so wonderful and so important for me to be around at that exact moment of my life. He and I met organically and unexpectedly and before we knew it, we were dating. He was a huge part of breaking my destructive cycle. He was so fun, so free, so present and so nurturing. I felt like I finally had a safe space to acknowledge all the nonsense swirling in my brain. I could talk about the emotional pain I had been repressing in order to maintain my absurd secret lifestyle. And it wasn't always a beautiful emotional release. It was hard and angry and sloppy and sad. But eventually I started to feel inspired.

The weirder my behavior got, the more private I became. And the more private I became, the weirder my behavior got.

Inspired by the world (in particular by comedy), inspired by life, and inspired to find out what would happen if I chose to think differently. (If you couldn't guess, my significant other also happened to be a psychology student—THANK GOD.)

So I started to make some changes. I started talking to people. To real therapists. To my family. But it was slow. And there were hiccups and regressions and difficulties. But still, it was progress. This is where I started bingeing on the stories of other people's struggles. I secretly bought books on Amazon about girls with EDs and I'd hide them under my mattress so my roommates wouldn't know (though I had begun to talk to people about my feelings, the bubble of people I spoke to was limited). The more I read, the more I felt less alone and less afraid and less completely crazy. There was finally some light at the end of that bleak, tired tunnel. I started taking chances. I took improv classes, I put together a sketch-comedy team on campus, I focused on other things that made me happy outside of the game.

Don't get me wrong: trying to heal myself definitely hasn't been an overnight process. It's slooooow. And though

I started to get a handle on my ED, it never completely leaves. It's like a scar that's faded but in a certain light becomes more visible.

After I graduated college, I moved to NYC and got more dedicated to pursuing comedy while auditioning for TV and film. The entertainment industry, just like modeling, has a tremendous focus on what you look like. And most of my auditions were for "sexy this" and "hot that," and I *hated* it. I could feel myself being triggered in waiting rooms by looking around at all the confident, beautiful, *skinny* actresses around me wearing tight tank tops and heels. And I never dressed like that. What I really wanted to wear to these auditions—oversized sweaters and leggings and Uggs (HOLLa aT ya, Jersey) because they made me feel the closest to "comfortable in my body"—would *never* get me cast. I remember wearing a slightly oversized, flowy button-down shirt and leggings to an audition for a really cool but of course *sexy* lead of a new ABC show and the casting lady (who was INCreDIBLY nice, to her credit) asked if I had a tank top with me that I could do the audition in instead. What I was wearing didn't look sexy enough on camera (spoiler: Hollywood *loves* clavicles). I reluctantly agreed and tried to push through the audition, but I was so wildly uncomfortable. I couldn't help feeling like I was exposing too much of myself and I was only wearing a tank top. I was so anxious I broke out in hives in the middle of it. I didn't book that one. In those moments I could feel the ED scar becoming a little more visible and I would become a little more doubtful.

Then I started to dabble in Web videos. There were no casting ladies sitting with me in my apartment while I made videos for the Internet. In those, I could wear whatever I wanted. And style my hair and makeup however I felt most comfortable. And I did. The Internet allowed me to express my personality rather than my cleavage. In my journey to body acceptance, it's become such an important and invaluable outlet for me.

It's been ten years since I first acknowledged to myself that my patterns of thought might possibly be f*cked up. And only recently, thanks a lot in part to the Internet, have I been able to feel most comfortable in my own skin. That's all skin is—just a sock puppet for our personality (a quote from a journal of mine in 2008).

And with that I'll wrap up my ED exposition portion of this book. Don't fear, this book isn't and was never meant to be an autobiography of my body issues. Nor is this an *actual* style guide. Oops. Sorry if you thought so. You got pranked so hard! What broke a lot of my unhealthy behavior was reading tough doses of reality mixed with the therapy of comedy and making light of my own darkness. And I know body and beauty issues are something so many of us struggle with, so hopefully this was helpful.

Now that the reality part is out of the way, let's dive into what I've come to acknowledge as one of the most hilarious subject matters in our society: beauty and style.

Over the years I've tried to turn my personal struggle into perspective, and now I really believe that beauty is completely comical. It's goddamn ridiculous. Fabrics and textiles can define us? The convex and concave shapes that make up our bodies can devalue us? The amount of skin you have on one of your eyelids can determine a career? So dumb!

Let's dive into what I've come to acknowledge as one of the most hilarious subject matters in our society: beauty and style.

So, friend/stranger/semi-familiar associate/AI robot, welcome to a style book unlike any you may have read before. Obviously, I don't know the "correct" way to do style, but I've discovered my way to try. And I'd like to share that with you. I hope you're willing. Please enjoy my stupid thoughts on the things I've learned along with some nonsensical analyses of glamour, fashion, and fads.

And hey, by the way, your eyelids look fantastic.

This might sound so dumb, but I have to tell you that I decided to write about my ED after going to a tarot-card reader. She's shockingly good and was so spot-on about a lot of things in my life that toward the end of my reading I asked her to pull a card for my book. I can't remember exactly which card she pulled, but she explained, with no knowledge of what kind of book I was writing, that I was going to have to pull back a curtain and reveal more of myself before my creative juices could flow and I could produce the kind of book I'd *really* want others to read. Welp, I feel like I just tore the curtains straight off the window. Sorry, curtains. But I gotta say, the sunshine coming through the window feels pretty great.

a few of my favorite things

Before we dive into my ideas and feelings about fashion, I thought it might be helpful to share some of my favorite things. Not only does this feed my narcissism, it also gives you a solid base of personal information to form judgments about me.

1. **Favorite Color:** stripes

2. **Favorite Shoes:** Uggs (I'll never be president, I GET IT.)

3. **Favorite Long-Term Piece of Clothing Owned:** a way-too-small seventies tennis sweatshirt and a green T-shirt I got in fifth grade that says "I'm a Terrific Kid"

4. **Favorite Kind of Night Out:** me + my couch + my sweatpants + my subtle sadness + my recently cleared to-do list + my stockpile of unwatched episodes of *Dance Moms* and *Real Housewives*

5. **Favorite Bag:** a navy-blue pleather backpack from ASOS

6. **Favorite Hairstyle:** messy, beachy waves that take way too long to look effortless

7. **Favorite City:** I love London and New York in medium doses

8. **Favorite Lip Product:** the grease left over from breakfast meats

9. **Favorite Season:** five o'clock

A FEW OF MY FAVORITE THINGS

10. **Favorite Hair Accessory:** dry shampoo

11. **Favorite Emoji:** that calm, pleasant-old-man face

12. **Favorite Store:** any store where the employees are too uninterested/hungover to ask me if I need help or to judge me for walking in circles when I get too over-whelmed by options

13. **Favorite Celebrity Style:** Emma Stone, the Hamburglar, *Where's Waldo?*, and russet potato bags

14. **Favorite Disney Character Style:** Prince Eric from *The Little Mermaid* (he had a classic look that I love: a chic white button-up and fitted jeans)

15. **Favorite Accessory:** a smile, SIKE; I like small, unexpected silly pieces (e.g., a French-bulldog ring, shoes with French fries on them, etc.)

16. **Favorite Style Moment:** Recently my friend Mamrie Hart and I performed a handful of live comedy shows dressed in spandex suits that were made to make us look like professional male wrestlers. Neither one of us has ever looked so toned.

17. **Favorite Mantra:** We're all going to die someday!

18. **Favorite Social Media Platform:** currently I'm big into Snapchat; it's silly and sloppy and unedited, a lot like my personal style

19. **Favorite Holiday:** I love New Year's Eve. I'm someone who subscribes to "fresh starts," "optimism," and "bullsh*t resolutions." And it's a bonus that you get to dress up as much or as little as you want for the night; NYE has a uniquely broad tolerance of fashion and f*ckery that I can't help but love.

20. **Favorite Thing to Hear You Say After Reading This Book:** "It wasn't the worst!"

grace

clothing...clothing...clothing...clothing

clothing...

The art of not being naked......The art of the advanced toga...

...The art of ruining your hair......The art of the body tarp

......The art of camouflaging your low self-confidence.........

clothing...clothing

.......The art of skin censoring.......

....The art of the everyday "human" Halloween costume.....

.......The art of the modern mummy........

.....The art of hanging your carcass curtains.........

The art of maintaining your full-body-napkin...

vintage grace

SHOPPING LESSONS FROM MY FATHER

When I was in sixth grade, the Limited Too was the shopping mecca.

Girls were made and betrayed by that innocent, bubble-letter font with the flower in the logo. If you shopped at Limited Too, you were hot sh*t. And probably too young to use the phrase "hot sh*t" colloquially.

For those of you unfamiliar, Limited Too was the teen/tween branch of the women's clothing store The Limited. It had all of the most colorful, trendsetting clothes an upper-middle-class suburban girl could dream of.

Growing up I could never afford to shop at the Limited Too. Instead, I was limited to Ross Dress for Less, Kohl's, and JCPenney. All very respectable, but they were the Taylor Swift circa 2011 to the Limited Too's Taylor Swift circa now. I watched all the popular girls (who all happened to play soccer) dominate off the field with their sweet sparkle-trimmed cardigans and perfectly plaid miniskirts. And that was just a regular school day; don't even get me started on what they wore to dances. When I went to middle-school dances I danced like no one was watching, because no one *was*—my outfits weren't as cute as the other girls' and didn't merit the attention. I tried to compete with my ill-fitting Calvin Klein button-up shirts that I got at Ross and my imitation mini-ish skirts I got from the DEB. If you're not familiar with DEB, it's like the trashy stepsister of Forever 21 that takes F21 out for her twenty-first birthday, pumps her full of Jell-O shots, and convinces her to get a bald-eagle tattoo. It's probably just a South Jersey thing, but you're probably familiar with DEB's boyfriend, Spencer's Gifts, or equally trashy BFF, 5-7-9? If you're not, I'm sure your mom is very proud of you.

From fifth through ninth grade, Limited Too was the unspoken divider between the middle-school spoiled royals and the rest of us regulars. You were either a girl who shopped there or you were a girl who shopped the six-for-the-price-of-one earrings at the Claire's across the way spying on the girls in LT hoping they might drop a $75 sweater-vest on their way out. Sidenote: Even though I desperately wanted to be a girl who shopped at LT, I still couldn't understand paying those prices. I'd spent too many years watching my mom use every kind of coupon/special credit card/frequent-buyer scratch-off card/random-discount lifeline to know those prices were stupid. I still believe that a store that doesn't allow you to scratch off a lottery ticket at the checkout for a chance at extra savings is an example of modern-day communism. Shout-out to my scratch-off dealer, Kohl's! And maybe that was part of the allure of LT. It didn't have to offer silly sales or money-saving gimmicks to sell clothes. You either bought their stupidly expensive clothes or you didn't. And I didn't.

UNTIL MY TWELFTH BIRTHDAY.

My dad has always been hilariously forgetful and unprepared when it comes to giving gifts. He waits until the very last minute and is never sure what to buy, so you can usually expect a slightly weird but well-intentioned present. One year he got my stepmom a framed picture of a rain forest for her birthday. She's never been to a rain forest. But she does wear a lot of animal-print clothing.

For my twelfth birthday (I was in seventh grade) my dad took me to the mall and told me I could spend $50 anywhere I wanted. In hindsight, this was probably a test to see if I'd choose the science store since he'd taken my younger brother and me there so frequently. But all I could think in that moment was, *How am I ever going to decide between the prep-school-inspired sweater-vests with sewn-in collared shirts or the pink plastic crop jackets?* LIMITED TOO, IT'S YOU AND ME . . . *and my dad.* (In reality my dad has a son with a master's from MIT, so at least someone in our family benefited from the science store.)

So my pops and I set off for my popular-making paradise. When we walked in, my ears were blessed with the hypnotic sounds of one Britney Spears and my nose was slapped with the scent of artificial vanilla. At that moment I realized IT'S VERY AWKWARD SHOPPING WITH YOUR FATHER. Did I forget to mention this was our first one-on-one shopping experience while I was in my quiet, awkward, I-don't-know-what-to-do-with-my-body-and-my-personality phase? My poor dad. The only other fashion experience we'd had together was when he tried to do my hair (pretty terribly) for Christmas when I was six and he was a single dad. My father did not understand the stylistic and social importance of the Limited Too. This was MY OLYMPICS. And conversely I did not understand how to shop with my dad. This was about to be an educational experience for both of us.

It began at an awkward pace. I, overwhelmed by being inside LT with ACTUAL intentions of purchasing something mixed with the unfamiliarity of how to shop with my dad, wandered around the store paralyzed by choices but touching everything. Sidenote: Why do we always TOUCH everything when we shop? Even if I'm in a store and I know it's too expensive and I don't plan on buying anything, I'll still touch a bunch of stuff thinking that equals "shopping." Imagine seventh-grade Grace touching *everything* while my dad touches *nothing* so as not to commit himself to needing help from a sales rep and/or looking like a childless pervert. Meanwhile, I'm wrapped up in my fantasy life trying to appear to the other girls shopping there that I know what I'm doing and I clearly shop here all the time and I definitely am not even considering the pathetic-looking sales rack tucked in the very back of the store where I could spread my wealth among more than one item, allowing me to show my peers that I own THINGS from Limited Too. *Things*. Plural.

I would never have this opportunity again so I had to make this purchase count.

Pssshhhh. Yeah, right. Not even considering it. I'll be over here touching a ton of pleather jackets. To put it lightly, I was freaking the f*ck out. There were too many options! I would never have this opportunity again, so I had to make this purchase count.

I scrambled my brain considering every unique feather-trimmed tank and bedazzled sweatsuit they offered. Touch touch touch touch. Velour sweatshirt? Touch. Maybe a denim skort. Touch. Touch. I could practically feel OCD developing.

Until my dad appeared. In an equally exhausted and overwhelmed state, he ushered me over to the front of the store to show me what he thought I should buy: jeans.

Jeans?!

I was in a store that was about to make me Cher from *Clueless* and he wanted me to buy Jeans?! That's like going to Old Country Buffet and getting a small salad and some water. My dad went on to explain to me, in his usual practical and articulate way, that he believed the jeans had a longer shelf life than any of the other items in the store. He also told me that even though the jeans were $54 he would cover the extra cost. Extra cost?! Jeans?! Looking back on it now, I think my dad felt strongly about the jeans because they were the only item in the store he could recognize and identify as "clothing."

I was so confused. Was my dad trying to sabotage my future rise to preteen middle-school queen? I didn't care how long the jeans lasted; I wanted to be popular now! And no one ogled the soccer girls' *jeans*. Jeans didn't stand out. Jeans didn't overcompensate. They didn't say "I'm interesting" the way the floral bodysuits did! I was so overwhelmed and tired and embarrassed that I finally just agreed and bought a pair of classic-fit straight-leg jeans for $54 plus tax. On the way home I felt so defeated. I had an opportunity to reach greatness and I settled for *jeans*. I blew it.

Cut to four years later, my dad knew it. For about four years I wore those classic-fit straight-leg jeans once a week, making my T.J. Maxx T-shirts look *good* and possibly tricking people into thinking I owned more than one pair. And they were the most comfortable pair of jeans I ever owned as an awkward, lanky, puberty-cursed teenager. Those jeans truly were a classic. They lasted for the long haul and stayed in style, until those damn bell-bottoms came back and dominated.

It also turned out that I was never going to be popular in high school. So thinking that some trendy pleather skirt was going to change everything was delusional. If there's one thing my dad knows how to do, it's procrastinate and stick to the basics. He's a simple man who doesn't need frills. Literally. Never once did he suggest investing in frilly lace shorts. My dad taught me the value of a classic. Clothes are like friends and fake plants: invest in the ones that will last. Thanks, Dad—your natural fight-or-flight instincts in a preteen clothing store accidentally taught me a core fashion lesson. Turns out, I'm not *limited to* trends. I'm so sorry.

Why be
a fashion
plate …
when
you can
be a
fashion
"dish"!

basics

WORK IT

I know the Ring Pop on the cover may have fooled you into thinking this is an informative style guide, but it's not. There are thousands of magazine articles, television shows, and books out there that can tell you the appropriate things to wear in the workplace, so we're going to skip all of that. Instead, I'd like to explore the things you *shouldn't* wear in the workplace. Because no one tells us that. And it's important. So important that I've compiled an extremely thorough list.

However! If you were really hoping to read actual advice about workplace staples, here's a quick overview: do not wear actual staples. Also, take these suggestions with a grain of salt; they're coming from a girl who is technically in her "workplace" right now, shoeless and wearing a lime-green T-shirt with giant ironed-on letters spelling out "grace." I am fashion.

HERE'S THE BORING LIST OF THINGS EVERYONE TELLS YOU TO WEAR TO WORK:

- Comfortable, classic shoes
- Pants/trousers
- Pencil skirts
- Modest dresses
- Blouses, shirts, and blazers

HERE ARE MY WORKPLACE GO-TOS

If you're at all curious, here are the real things I wear to work. I work in a variety of settings. I work from home, I work on sets, I work from hotel rooms, I take meetings in coffee shops, offices, etc., etc., etc. My "professional" wardrobe varies depending on the work environment, but I usually opt for one of three looks:

→ Clean pants (jeans or otherwise), a (hopefully) stain-free top (T-shirt or button-down), maybe a statement necklace, some heels or ballet flats, and usually a leather bag

→ A shift dress or loose tunic with sneakers, ballet flats, or heels, and a leather backpack or clutch (only if I'm feeling wildly secure and not like I need to bring everything I own with me in case every emergency happens at once. I don't carry clutches often.)

→ Sweatpants, whatever shirt I slept in last night, and chip crumbs

Enough about me! Let's talk about things you shouldn't put on your person in the workplace (most obvious: your boss).

WHAT NOT TO WEAR TO WORK

A cardboard box: Yes, boxy can be fashionable, but a cardboard box isn't the best way to go. From personal experience I can tell you it's uncomfortable and can bruise the armpits and neck areas. Turns out people don't like it if you use the handicapped stall when you're not disabled. The color isn't flattering on most skin tones. And if you happen to spill any liquids on it, the smell of wet cardboard isn't helpful in a work environment. Leave the cardboard boxes at home, people!

Tinfoil: Modern/futuristic shapes and textures are fun to play with, but tinfoil will spoil the fun. It doesn't breathe, the edges are sharp, and don't even TRY to get near a microwave with it on. Eesh.

Chain mail: Unless you work at Medieval Times, chain mail isn't great for the office. It's loud, it's heavy, and it's really outdated. Stick to email. нananananananananana!

Toilet paper: Wearing toilet paper in the workplace is something no one tells you not to do, but you definitely shouldn't do it. In certain kinds of lighting it can be unexpectedly see-through (yikes!) and the durability factor is pretty low. It's not flattering to most body types and can end up giving you a bulkier shape than you actually have. Major fashion faux pas!

Candle wax: Yes, Ricky Martin has made candle wax a cool thing to put on your body, and yes, candle wax is cheap in bulk, but that still doesn't mean it's a good fit for the office. The potency of the scent can be difficult to regulate throughout the day, and if anyone happens to spill hot coffee on you, the wax will melt and it's game over. You won't look like a scene from a Ricky Martin music video. You'll look like a failed performance-art piece. And it's hard to negotiate a raise from your boss like that.

Live snakes: Live snakes, though extremely sexy for Britney Spears, are not appropriate for the workplace. They can be offensive, they molt, they're distracting, they're poisonous, Samuel L. Jackson hates them, you get it. Save the snakes for the weekend.

Fruit: Miss Chiquita Banana, the first lady of fruit, looks excellent in a fruit-filled headdress. But the rest of us, sadly, do not. A headpiece like that can give you neck cramps, it can attract bugs (and not just Phil from legal—nailed it!), and it can also be offensive and uncomfortable for anyone in the office with a pineapple allergy.

Fall Out Boy posters: By the time you've scored your full-time job, it's safe to say you've probably outgrown posters, so it's best to leave them at home. Especially the Fall Out Boy ones. They can cause paper cuts, they tear easily, and they can remind people of the dark time when Pete Wentz was married to Ashlee Simpson.

Glue: Glue is great for a lot of things, but not for wearing to work. It's tacky.

Jetpack: Trust me, I love jetpacks as much as the next guy, but they can be a bit risqué for the office. It depends what kind of shoes you wear with them, but to me they're a little too dressy. At the end of the day you want your work wardrobe to play a supporting role to your ideas and work ethic, not steal focus. Not everyone can pull off a jetpack, but if you're one of the lucky ones, save it for the office holiday party.

Water: I know everyone says they should have more water in their lives, but sorry to be the bearer of bad news, water as work wear is the wrong choice. It's a natural resource that needs protecting, it can be extremely see-through under fluorescent lighting, and your coworkers might mistake you for a water cooler and try to gossip near you. Save yourself the hassle.

Meat: This goes in line with the fruit. There's a time and a place to wear meat, but the workplace isn't one of them, unfortunately. Sorry if that rubs you the wrong way. Hot dogs!

A mascot costume: Unless you work as said mascot, it's best not to wear a mascot costume to work. They can start office arguments if your coworkers are fans of the opposing team. They can limit your peripheral vision, they can make typing and using the bathroom more difficult, and they can inspire unwanted associates to open up to you about their furry fetish. Best to save the costume for the tailgate this weekend.

A family member's ashes: A lot of people have sentimental items they wear to quietly remind themselves of people or places or things. And though they're excellent for contouring, ashes are most flattering in an urn rather than on your person.

Spices: Spices, like cinnamon and oregano, aren't optimal work attire. They can be very uncomfortable and can trigger allergies in coworkers. They also don't cover your private sectors, which may lead to your being fired. Paprik-ah geez. Orega-oh no.

Your emotions: You never want to wear your emotions on your sleeve or on yourself at the office. Keep them close to the vest. Or better yet, just wear the vest and pretend the emotions don't exist.

basics

GOING OUT

Getting dressed to go out is *always a process.*

You're dressing to impress and/or investing in potentially becoming a hot mess. The options are endless. Do you go sexy, elegant, classic, edgy, or casual? Everyone has opinions on the optimal going-out outfits. If you've been frozen in ice for decades and recently thawed, here are some of those usual suspects.

HERE'S THE BORING LIST OF THINGS EVERYONE TELLS YOU TO WEAR TO GO OUT:

- Party dresses
- Fancy pants/leggings
- Tight jeans
- Blouses
- Heels
- Jackets and coats

HERE ARE MY GOING-OUT GO-TOS

I like to keep things basic. If I decide to leave the safe, warm glow of my computer screen and venture into the real world after dark, it's usually to some sort of bar/restaurant-with-friends scenario, and less often to some sort of live-show/networking activity, and even less frequently to some sort of red-carpet event. Still, I usually opt for one of three looks:

✦ A pair of decently clean, decently fitted skinny jeans, a T-shirt or sweater, a statement necklace and/or stacks of rings, booties or ballet flats, and possibly a leather jacket

✦ A romper with some sneakers or heels (or heeled sneakers)

✦ A dress that someone else chose and dressed me in with shoes that someone else chose and put on my feet

Enough about me! Let's talk about the things you should put on your person when you go out for the night (most obvious: your boss).

WHAT NOT TO WEAR TO GO OUT

Plants: Plants are not a good choice to wear for an evening out. They're very itchy and can attract bugs and overeager DIY enthusiasts. Yes, air plants are all over Pinterest, but that doesn't mean they should be all over you. You're a wallflower; don't *wear* wallflowers. Also, I highly suggest avoiding wearing plants to a wedding or a frat party, as they're usually the first place drunk guests look to throw up into.

Wallpaper: Wallpaper, although fun, quirky, and expressive, is a no-no for nights out. The material definitely doesn't breathe well, especially if you end up dancing and/or in a humid environment. It can also create an unflattering body shape and any sweating can cause stickage. One zoo-themed wallpaper ensemble plus one hot nightclub dance floor will give a whole new meaning to the term "*camel* toe."

Scissors: I know it's next to impossible to stay away from scissors as part of a late-night getup. But you should try. You never know if your night will have you running for a taxi to stop the wedding of your one true love, running from a murderer who disguised himself as a seemingly perfect Tinder date, or just plain running with the devil. And running with scissors is extremely dangerous. So sacrifice looking *sharp* and leave the scissors at home.

Pizza and/or cookie dough: Any uncooked dough is definitely a do(ugh)n't! It can attract animals, depressed girls, and children. None of which you should have around you for an evening out.

Lawn furniture: Lawn furniture at tailgating events makes sense, but lawn furniture when you're out at night trying to get some tail is a fashion offense. It's best not to wear anything that might invite someone you're attracted to to "sit on you." Also any moisture (rain, tears, etc.) can cause rust. And my grandma always said, "Save the rusty nails for when you need to give yourself tetanus to get out of a lawsuit that was definitely your fault to begin with."

Tanks: Army tanks are never cute to wear out. They're very polarizing and aggressive and hard to do any "back dat ass up" in.

Spaghetti straps: Straps made from spaghetti look chic, but don't last. They fall apart, can cause unflattering odors, and attract stoners and raccoons. Instead, try other materials like papier-mâché or burlap.

Car parts: Car parts, though very urban and industrial, can get really cumbersome for a night out on the town. Like the men I date, they can be old, heavy, loud, gassy, and greasy. *Steer* clear of the car parts. LOL! Zoom!

Board games: Yes, board games are usually crowd favorites. But save them for game night. On a table. As an outfit, they can be bulky and incite arguments. Take a lesson from *NSYNC: the song is "Quit Playing Games WITH My Heart" not "Quit Playing Games ON My Heart." You want to *take* a risk with your nighttime look, not *wear* Risk as your nighttime look.

Balloons: Balloons are tricky business if you're going out for the night. They seem fun and festive but they're dangerous to dress up in. You have to be extra cautious of women and men with sharp jewelry and/or a fear of balloons. As an adult, I realize that I hate the experience of a balloon popping. It's a disgusting, immoral experience. Why create that scenario for others? Pop bottles, not balloons.

Your heart on your sleeve: Hearts belong in bodies so they can keep you alive. Do not put them on your sleeve.

Crop tops: Wearing crops for tops seems cute in theory, but in reality, they're inconvenient. Pesticides should be reason enough to avoid them. And if you're in harvest season, forget it, the ensemble becomes a total chore. Ew! Stick to organic materials.

Fajitas: Fajitas, while they do attract attention and are a suburban-family favorite, should be avoided for an evening ensemble. You've seen fajitas getting served in a chain restaurant, right? The obnoxious billowing smoke that follows them as a server brings them to a table? They're a direct reflection of the person ordering them. They practically scream, "LOOK AT ME, I'M INSECURE AND OVERCOMPENSATING." You don't need that in your late-night look. They say where there's smoke, there's fire. In this case, where there's smoke, there's third-degree burns because fajitas are too hot to put on your skin.

Season/series finale spoilers: Wearing a TV show's season or series finale spoiler is annoying and hateful and may cause people who've never hurt anyone in their lives to want to cut you. Especially if you wear spoilers to the most recent season of *RuPaul's Drag Race*. Stop that.

Always
try to
dress
like
you're
worth a
million
bucks
even
if your
net
worth
is only
a dollar
fifty.

MOM'S WORDS OF WISDOM

Monday, Sept. 14, 2015

Dear Diary,

Tomorrow is the day. It's my first day of ninth grade and my first day in a REAL SCHOOL *ever*! I'm sooooo nervous; it's really making me sweat! Sorry, Diary, you know one of my symptoms of stress is accidental pun-age. And I know *you* know this already, Diary, but if anyone else were to accidentally find this diary in the future and need some story context to be able to completely enjoy the variety of antics that surround my life, here ya go, stranger:

Until now, I've only ever been homeschooled because my SweatMom and SweatDad couldn't be bothered to get off their stupid beanbags to take me to a REAL school. It's all I've ever wanted. Growing up, I'd watch Gap and Old Navy commercials and just imagine myself in a class like that, with all the colors and conformity. *Sigh*, what a dream. You see, a lot of sweatpants like me never get a chance to go to school, and if we do, it usually ends up being a trade school like Sports Authority or Champs or, even worse, a DICK's Sporting Goods. Ugh! It makes me want to rip out my elastic waistband just thinking about it. But this year, I got lucky! For my fourteenth birthday, my grandma Windbreaker gave me the greatest gift EVER, an acceptance letter to THE MALL OF AMERICA. I nearly ripped a hole in my crotch opening the envelope, I was so excited! The Mall of America is one of the largest and most prestigious schools for wardrobe wannabes in the country! It's the capital of clothing, the UN of undergarments, the Ivy League of investing in a future that's sure to fit. Sorry, Diary! It's from the commercial!

I couldn't believe Grandma Windbreaker got me in! I asked her how in the world she did it and she pulled me aside and said she found the hidden stash of tests and writing samples I kept in my off-brand duffel bag under my generic wood-framed twin bed with Dallas Cowboys bedding. (I wanted a vintage cream quilt like the one I saw on Pinterest, but my Sweat-Dad wouldn't let me get it, he thought it was "too splashy." Let it be known, if it isn't a hot dog or ankle weights, it's probably *too splashy* for my SweatDad.)

Anyways, I was so embarrassed that G-Wind found my private papers! You see, I've been secretly taking some classes online at eBay.com and doing some practice essays I found in a forum on Overstock.com in the hopes that I might be able to convince my pant-rents to let me enroll in a school, ANY SCHOOL, by eleventh or twelfth grade so I'd *at least* have a year or two of store-study. But I had no idea it could happen this quickly!

G-Wind also got really serious and began to tell me a story I had never heard before. Appar(el)ently (sorry, D!) her SweatMom "Eliza Doolittle'd" (whatever that means) a business suit with money into marrying her and together they gave birth to my G-Wind. Evidently, BusinessDad was disappointed with her the second she was born. Because she was born a Windbreaker and not a suit like him and the rest of his dry-clean-only family. Tensions ran up like a hole in a pair of stockings and her SweatMom and BusinessDad eventually split at the seams.

Her SweatMom decided to take her settlement money and do all she could to make G-Wind's childhood better than her own, including sending her to the MOA. Trust me, I had *no idea* my G-Wind had gone there! But I've always thought my G-Wind was the smartest person I know, so it totally makes sense. She went on to tell me that her experience at the MOA was not a pleasant one. Uh-oh. Supposedly my G-Wind had a mouth that couldn't be zipped when she was younger. And the suits that ran the school, she said, reminded her of her BusinessDad who discarded her, so she started acting out. She'd get into arguments with uptight teachers and buttoned-up store managers until she ended up walking out of class. She couldn't stand being labeled and departmentalized. The school felt so Wind-resistant that she decided to start a protest group called "The Mall Walkers of America." Every Friday they'd meet before the school opened and walk the premises as a sign of peaceful protest. The administration hated it, but there was nothing they could do about it. Until the day the Mall Walkers were shut down. G-Wind called it Black Friday. She wouldn't give me too many details about the day, but said the protest escalator-ed and she was kicked out of the MOA for good. Her SweatMom was devastated. All that money... waisted.

She glazed over the specifics of what happened after she left the MOA, but in broad strokes she moved back in with her SweatMom, eventually went on to marry her late husband, my grandpa Windbreaker, they had my SweatMom, and lived a pretty generic life. She explained that because my SweatMom never showed any interest in *anything* other than covering herself in Cheetos stains growing up (no surprise), she hadn't even thought about the MOA until she came across my secret stash. She says she was in my room looking for her pull (if you aren't familiar, a pull is the metal tab on a zipper, it's common for olds to lose theirs fairly frequently), but if you ask me, I think she was hoping to find anything drug-related that would numb her to the reality TV my pant-rents watch every day. Sorry, G-Wind, you got yourself a pretty tapered SweatGranddaughter.

She said that when she found my tests and essays, she had a flashback to her younger, overly studious self. She said she knows I have real potential and she isn't going to let it go to waist.

And to be honest, Diary, that was the first time anyone has ever said that they believe in

Grace's blue Puma sweatpants

me. It made me feel elastic. Sorry, ecstatic. It made me feel ecstatic!

G-Wind said she had to pull some strings to get me in. She showed my scores and samples to Dr. Scholls, who she mentioned was an old friend of hers who teaches at the school, and he passed them on to the Brooks Brothers, the legendary superintendents of the MOA and the ones who kicked G-Wind out of the school for good that infamous Black Friday long ago. Because of that, she had to have Dr. Scholls present the scores as if they were from his own SweatGranddaughter, which she says was a very dangerous and generous thing for him to do. And I don't even know the guy! Makes me wonder...

Wondering over! Evidently the Brothers were very impressed with my work, and though they hardly ever allow sweatpants (or the like) into their academy, they would make an exception on account of Dr. Scholls's long-lasting loyalty to the MOA. Sheesh, I feel like I owe this guy my sole.

With that, G-Wind said she was finished blabbering on about the past. She wanted to talk about my future. She rested her thin, wrinkled sleeves on me and told me that she wants me to succeed. She wants me to have the life her SweatMom tried to give her. She said, "You take the MOA by (Wind) storm and show 'em the only thing sloppy about you is your handwriting."

And she's right, I have very sloppy penmanship.

She hugged me close and continued: "The only thing you need to do is make sure no one knows you're related to me. As far as the BBs know, you're Dr. Scholls's SweatGranddaughter twice restocked, and that's all anyone needs to know." Before I could even question the statement, she started playing Britney Spears's "Work Bitch" on her iWatch and shuffled out of my room, hands in the air like she was victorious, crossing a finish line.

And now here I am, Diary. The night before I leave for the MOA. My mind is a gymnasium of thoughts and emotions. My duffel bags are packed and the only thing I know is that Dr. Scholls is supposed to meet me when I arrive to help get me settled. But what if he doesn't show up? What if I end up in the Lost and Found? Should I try to iron myself again? Do I have everything? Do I have my drawstrings, my stain sticks, should I brush up on my folding??? ACK!

But as manic as I seem, Diary, know that I'm just as excited. I'm starting a brand-new life! At the MOA! THE MOA! Ahhhhhh! I still can't believe it. It's going to be great! Okay, I'm gonna try to get to sleep. Wish me luck, D! Cheers to a new adventure! (Trust me, I tried to think of a pun to end this, but my brain is just too tied up right now—HEYO!)

Love,
Sweatpants

style staples and fashion favorites

FREQUENT AND QUESTIONABLE (FAQs)

I realize one of the major components of writing a beauty book is sharing your personal sense of style. So I wanted to give you a quick look at some of my style staples and fashion favorites. I guarantee that once you go through these, you'll wonder who could have possibly given me the green light to write a style guide, and if they are still employed. The answers are "an actual human" and hopefully "yes!" Let's look at my preferred apparel. I call them my FAQs because they're Frequent And Questionable.

Stripes: Stripes have been a staple of mine for years. This shirt isn't my favorite in particular (sorry, this shirt!), but it is representative of my extensive collection of striped clothing. I think stripes are classic and casual, relaxed and refined. They can act as a neutral and be worn with a lot of different color combinations, or they can be worn with a more toned-down palette and make a bold statement. To me they feel timeless, genderless, and effort- less: three qualities I really love in clothing. For some reason I've always been attracted to neutral color palettes and more nautical- or Americana-inspired patterns. (Appar- ently, I was in the navy in a past life? Or I'm just desperately trying too hard to be Reese Witherspoon in this current life?) I seem to always have at least five to ten differ- ent, inexpensive striped T-shirts, sweat- ers, and dresses in rotation in my closet because I wear them constantly and gross them up consistently. The only thing in my life I've ever been consistent about is an inconsistent level of cleanliness.

Cozy Sweater: Neutral-
colored, slightly oversized sweaters have always been a love of mine. I like my sweat- ers like I like my men—not clingy and kinda sloppy. I keep a few different col- ors on hand—creams, beiges, dark greens, navy blues, grays, and blacks mostly. I'm sorry if this sounds like a *Goop* newsletter,

but I honestly love the look of cozy sweaters with shorts. It's impossible not to say or type the words "cozy sweaters" without seeming like a cozy asshole. Regardless, for me the sweater-and-shorts combo is like tater tots and cake frosting: delicious separately, addictive together, and sometimes misunderstood. Such clothes have the timeless, genderless, and ageless trinity I look for in most of the things I wear, and a lot of times they're easier for me to throw on and keep track of throughout the night than a jacket. All in all, I feel better in my sweaters.

Sweatpants: Well, this should be the biggest "no duh" of all time, but if you don't know already, one of my fashion favorites is sweatpants. Damn, I love me a sweet pair of sweats. I've always loved comfortable clothing. Right after I graduated college, I went through a phase of constantly wearing leggings and my BF's oversized collared button-downs. It was my go-to combo when going out to bars, going on auditions, and appearing onstage. For some reason I thought the combo looked hipster-cute and trendy without trying. And on a lot of other girls in Brooklyn it did. But when I look back at photos of myself wearing it, I look like I'm wearing an Ina Garten Halloween costume.

Don't get me wrong; Ina is a style icon. But I can't pull this look off as well as she can. Every once in a while I give it another try, but I never look as timeless, genderless, and effortless as the Barefoot Contessa.

But that's where sweatpants come in! Stylish sweatpants, or "joggers"—as uptight fashionistas refer to them in an effort to separate them from sweatpants even though they are very much sweatpants—have become a huge trend in the fashion world and have fulfilled the tasteful-lazy void in my life post-leggings. I currently own probably fifteen pairs of fancy sweatpants and can't walk out of a store without almost buying two more. I'm sure I'll have the same thoughts about them in hindsight as I have about the leggings/button-down combo, but for now I'm letting myself believe they're easy, breezy, stylish, and cheeky. They make me feel like Gwen Stefani, even if in reality I look like Al Bundy. Either way, I'll take it!

Jumpsuit: Currently my must-haves for formal affairs are jumpsuits and rompers. They're like dresses but safer, or like two-piece suits but lazier. And I love them. Yes, they're extremely risky and complicated for public bathroom scenarios, but we take all kinds of gross risks when we use public restrooms period. In my opinion, rompers and jumpsuits are both unassuming and eye-catching. My aesthetic for elegant events is "sexy car mechanic" or "sophisticated ghostbuster," and that's exactly what rompers and jumpsuits deliver. For me they take a lot of the guesswork out of putting together

an outfit but still manage to look like I put in some time and effort with my ensemble. I'm a disillusioned illusionist; my style is primarily simple items that trick you into thinking they're more sophisticated (like when you only read one chapter of every Malcolm Gladwell book just so you can pretend to talk about them at parties since everyone *loves* talking about Malcolm Gladwell books).

Graphic Tees: As of late, graphic T-shirts have been the real foundation of my fashion. They're the closest I'll get to expressing my emotions in public. They're also a clear sign that I'm trying to hold on to any available youth I have left. Again, like my other style staples, one of their most redeeming qualities is that they're cheap and easy. But an added benefit with these buddies is that you can make your own even cheaper and easier (see: the future DIY section about restoring your boring T-shirts). Lately I've been a huge proponent of opposites; I love balancing a casual graphic shirt with a more polished leather skirt, or balancing a plain pocket tee with a fitted pair of black pants and heels, or even balancing an endless mountain of work with an extremely distracting *RuPaul's Drag Race* marathon. Life is about finding harmony.

OUTERWEAR
AND
UNDERWEAR

Whether you know it or not, outerwear and underwear have a lot in common:

1. They serve practical functions outside of simply being stylish.

2. They protect sensitive parts of your body against the elements.

3. They can make you feel like a completely different person.

4. You don't *always* need to wear them when you go out.

5. A true significant other keeps an eye on them for you at social events.

6. It's okay to upgrade them every year.

7. This is kind of embarrassing to include, but don't be afraid to purchase the pieces that might make you feel sexy. Eep! It can be fun and empowering on a private, personal level.

8. As you get older, you learn the benefit of investing in higher-quality versions of them: turns out they last longer, even in the most extreme conditions.

9. No matter how sophisticated you might feel as an adult, don't throw away those old "in case of emergency" pieces: you'll need them.

10. Do *not* forget to pack them when you travel. Your mother or grand-mother will inevitably ask about them, and it's a real bitch being without them when you don't know how far away the closest Target might be.

11. If they're more complicated to clean than you assume, then you should probably clean them more often than you do.

12. They make decent impromptu hairnets/umbrellas if you get caught in the rain.

13. Make sure you have them before you start your walk of shame. DON'T leave them at a stranger's place.

"A woman's dress should be like a barbed-wire fence: serving its purpose without obstructing the view."
—SOPHIA LOREN

"A woman's dress should be like a barbed-wire fence: it keeps the prisoners from escaping."
—GRACE HELBIG

dear miss mess

Optimistically speaking, we're all whirling dervishes

of potential disaster. Physically, emotionally, spiritually, and wardrobe-ally. At the same time we're all bedraggled tools of potential disaster relief. We f*ck up. We fix it. It's the circle of life. Just ask that emotionally-unstable-yet-very-lithe-for-his-age monkey from *The Lion King*.

And when it comes to disaster, our clothing is no exception. At this point in my life, my ability to accidentally defile my outfit has reached an all but spiritual level. I consider myself a practicing Christain. And, trust me, this is a very popular religion. Janet Jackson and Fergie have done some great work spreading the word of the Church of Wardrobe Malfunction. In this faith, R.I.P. has a HOLE new meaning. Get it? Rip? Hole? Like you rip a hole in your . . . okay, mass has ended, go in pieces.

But on another, philosophical level, the world revolves around the cycle of destruction *and* creation! That means every fashion affliction has a chance of being reborn *reworn*. I'LL STOP.

We all face unexpected wardrobe malfunctions. So allow me, Miss Mess, to offer you some advice that might remedy what's been wrecked and fix what you f*cked up. May these answers lead you to everlasting eterKNITy. SIKE, I Can'T STOP.

Dear Miss Mess,

This morning I was rushing into my office building ten minutes late. I was late because I had *that* dream about Jon Stewart again. I wrote to you about it last week in my "cargo pants OH no" email (which ended up working out fine because I found another pocket in my pants where I could keep the cake). *Anyway*, if you forgot, every week I have a dream that starts off with me bumping into Jon Stewart in a Chipotle and ends with him paying the extra cost for my guac. This dream's sexual innuendo is what should cost extra, I'll tell you that much. If you have thoughts on what it means, that'd be great, but it's not my primary question.

I was in such a rush this morning that I threw on a pair of Banana Republic trousers. Yes, I own clothing from Banana Republic. I'm really impressive, I know. But I'm also super economical; I got these pants for 70 percent off last summer because the waist is twisted and there's an extra pocket on the hip. I thought they had potential and that I could fix them. I even signed up for a sewing class a couple weeks after I bought them, but I walked out of the first lesson because the old woman next to me kept complimenting me on my natural ability at the sewing machine. I knew she was either being sarcastic or she was trying to win me over with praise so I would help her get to her car or something after class and then slowly start

These pants look totally fine... if I never raise my arms above my waist and if no one looks at me below my neck all day.

asking me week-to-week to do more and more things for her until we were in some weird pseudo-grandmother/granddaughter relationship and that's NOT what I signed up for.

Anyway, I didn't need the class because these pants look totally fine with a belt and a long cardigan, if I never raise my arms above my waist and if no one looks at me below my neck all day.

But the problem is, people look at me a lot all day because I have a very striking nose and I wheeze a lot. You see, the air that blows from our building's air-conditioning system is extra dry and I have NUMEROUS emails out to the owner of our building about it but he won't reply to them because I'm almost positive he's involved in the Persian mafia and the air-conditioning units are what they use to smuggle their drugs and he doesn't want me to find out. I'm like 80 percent sure.

Drugs aside, my bigger problem today is that I forgot to grab my belt. And the long cardigan I brought with me is completely wrinkled. Which brings up a long-standing question I have about how sweaters get wrinkles. You'd think their thickness would keep them wrinkle resistant. I think the Downy Wrinkle Releaser people have invested in something that gets mixed in with sweater fabrics and causes the garments to wrinkle so that the Downy company can keep the demand for their product high. Everyone's corrupt. Also, sidenote, do you know anyone who knows Jon Stewart? I get a feeling you're well connected. Let me know.

Anyway, I got to the office building this morning and sprinted into the elevator, and it smelled like musty onions because Kevin the janitor was already inside eating an everything bagel. Every morning he rides the elevators up and down and eats an everything bagel while he watches highlights from *The View* on his flip phone. Kevin is a huge Whoopi fan. He dresses up like her for Halloween every year. It's creepy, but he's one of those people I make sure to be nice to because there's a 60 percent chance be might kill me. He's got a face like that.

But when I got into the elevator and I smelled the stupid onions, it reminded me that I was supposed to sit in on a meeting my boss had set up with Henry Bagel, the inventor and CEO of Go-Gurt, to map out a digital campaign for their new savory pizza and pasta flavors. Which is a huge misstep for their product if you ask me, but then again, the invention of their product is a huge misstep for the snack industry in general if you ask me.

The meeting was supposed to be happening in five minutes. You can't even eat a burrito with extra guac in five minutes! Then I remembered that extra guac was part of my Stewart sex dream and that sex dream is what made me late and caused me to end up in a pair of deformed pants with an ugly sweater! I couldn't possibly be in a meeting with Henry Bagel looking like that! It's Henry Bagel! Yes, his product is of questionable taste, but his sense of style is spot-on. The man makes Calvin Klein look like *Calvin and Hobbes*. It's wildly ironic. But my time was running out. My first thought was that if I could make it to the boardroom before everyone else, I could choose a seat that kept me covered from the waist down for most of the meeting.

But that won't work!

Cheryl the intern (she has a forehead tattoo) *always* gets to meetings before everyone else. I'm like 75 percent sure it's because she made an irresponsible young-adult decision to get the forehead tattoo, so now she lives in a world of overcompensating in order to make herself seem somewhat responsible. To be fair, the forehead tattoo is a star and it's extremely stupid.

The elevator kept going up and up and I was scrambling to think of some way I could make it to the meeting on time. Finally it hit the ninth floor and the doors opened. I pushed past Kevin, but not before he said to me, "It'll get better." I asked what he meant and he pointed at my pants and said, "I make my own pants, too. The first couple times are the hardest. But I am LIVING FOR that secret side pocket. It's perfect for pickles and cigarettes." And then the elevator doors closed.

There weren't enough hours in the workday for me to completely process what he'd just said or try to erase the image in my mind of him sitting pantless at a sewing machine. So I raced to my desk to find a message saying the meeting had been pushed back a half hour. Which gave me enough time to write this email to you rather than trying to find the closest clothing store in order to possibly buy a new outfit. In hindsight, I feel I've made terrible use of my time, and now I have only fifteen minutes left before the meeting. I'll be sitting here refreshing my in-box over and over hoping you respond immediately rather than attempting to find a solution on my own. Again, I don't believe that's the greatest decision I should make for myself, but there's no going back. What should I do? Help!

Sincerely,

Frumpy Dumpy from Wall, New Jersey

—

Dear Frumpy Dumpy,

Looks like you got yourself in a real pickle. And not the kind Kevin likes. Though he seems great. First of all, no, I do not know anyone who knows Jon Stewart, and if I did, I'm 99 percent sure I would not introduce them to you. And definitely not because you're severely neurotic and wobbly in the emotional stability department, but because I believe dreams are sometimes better than reality. So go on with your spicy Chipotle sex dreams.

In regards to your outfit, here's what I think your options might be.

You could, **ONE**, **ask for help**. You could talk to that guy whose name you don't know—all you know is that he's the quiet, shy guy who drank an entire bowl of Jell-O shots at the office's nondenominational holiday party and tried to lick the inside of your ear because it looked like a "small vagina" . . . maybe it didn't happen exactly that way for you, but every office has that guy: the quiet guy. And I'm sure you think he has an extensive plan to kill you, but he's actually just waiting for you to start a conversation with him first. But I'm fairly certain that won't happen. Try asking him to let you borrow the oversized cardigan that he keeps on his desk chair. If you add that to your ensemble instead of the wrinkled cardigan, you can make it look like you're a hip, young creative type who loves shopping for vintage clothes and mixing and matching old and new (like you and Jon Stewart). You're an artist. You're innovative. Preppy is out, schleppy is in.

Goooooo, Go-Gurt!

Also, I'm assuming the meeting shouldn't take longer than an hour, so you shouldn't break out in too many unwashed-sweater-induced rashes before it's over. And you sound like the kind of person who keeps a variety of ointments nearby in case of emergency anyway.

You could, *two*, **creatively convert**. Does your purse have a detachable handle? Awesome. Use it as a belt! And if your burrito bliss caused you to forget your purse altogether, then today's the day you sweeten up Cheryl to see if she might be able to help you out. She's got a forehead tattoo; therefore, I assume she's got to have some sort of oversized puffed-rice hemp necklace or something at her desk. See if you can use that to cinch the waist. Meanwhile, gather the excess fabric on the ill-fitting button-down you decided was "good enough for today" in the back and staple it together to give yourself some shape. Then either tie your cardigan with the corporately induced wrinkles around your waist or over your shoulders

> "If I'm going dancing, then I wear the highest heels with the shortest dress."
> —KATE MOSS

> "If I'm going dancing, I stay away from high expectations and hope to spend only a short time at the dance club."
> —GRACE HELBIG

to conceal the staples. That or just take a trip down to the Lost and Found and see what helpful treasures may be lurking there.

You could, **three**, **alter the scenario**. If no one's willing to help you out, why not create an elaborate story about the trials and tribulations you have endured since agreeing to be a model in a *Project Runway* rip-off clothing-design competition reality show. You thought it would be a "fun time," but it turned out that the episode you were in was the one in which the designers' pets made the outfits for them. Unfortunately you got teamed up with a man named Guy whose French bulldog gave zero sh*ts about accentuating anything but the amount of followers on his Instagram account, and thus you ended up in the atrocity Mr. Bagel will soon see before him. And if you smell like piss (polite laugh), that's obviously from THE DOG.

You could, **four**, **own it**. Embrace your haphazard sloppiness. It's what makes you a human. So what, you were running late this morning . . . it happens to everyone! The people at the meeting don't need to know your *salsa specifics*. What you're wearing was unfortunately the only thing you had around that was even close to clean. Make a joke of it. You're self-aware, and that's charming. But in your haste to get ready for work this morning, the one thing you wish you'd had readily available, more than an ironed sweater, is a quick, satisfying meal on the run. You don't know, maybe something like a SAVORY GO-GURT. UH-OH, SLAM DUNK. Your hot-mess-ness now becomes the hot ticket into the psyche of the young, entrepreneur types Mr. Bagel should be marketing his new products to. TAKE THAT, CHERYL.

Hope this wasn't the worst advice in the whole goddamn world.

Sincerely,
Miss Mess

Dear Miss Mess,

The night started with me and my roommates passing around some sh*tty plastic-bottled tequila while we got ready to head out the door to Kevin Spacey's white party. Not, like, the actor Kevin Spacey. Kevin Spacey is the guy in my women's studies class with the sexy jawline and one huge calf, no one knows why, I think his mom drank a lot of Red Bull when she was pregnant. Every year Kevin and his roommate throw a white party in the crappy house they rent off campus. Apparently it started as a Walter White party, but no one read the Facebook invite, so everyone just showed up wearing white and it became a white party.

I left my other white shirts in the washer overnight and now they smell like wet cardboard.

I'm wearing my H&M white jeans and a man's white T-shirt I bought an hour ago at a CVS because I left my other white shirts in the washer overnight and now they smell like wet cardboard. It's not my fault my stupid mom never taught me how to do my laundry. Well, she tried to teach me one time, but I had to go to T.G.I. Friday's with my friends instead for Krista's birthday. And my mom definitely knew that because she stalks my Facebook constantly to see if I'm doing drugs.

Anyways, me and my dorm mates, the twins Ava and Eva (a lot of people at my school have super-unfortunate names), walked out to our Uber and Ava kept complaining that she ate too much guacamole before we left and Eva kept yelling at her because she knows guac causes Ava to make ass-ripping farts. They're so annoying. The twins, not the farts. Wait, no, actually the farts are stupid annoying, too.

We got to the parking lot and there was a wood-paneled station wagon with a super-old lady named Carol driving it. We totally freaked because if we got in the car with her, we were gonna look like nerds who got their mom to drive them to the party. And I'm sure my mom probably definitely already knew about this party because she's always on my Facebook! Goddammit, Mom!

Anyways, before we could cancel the trip, Carol yelled at us, "You Ava and Eva? Y'all look hot, you're going to Spacey's, right? Get in, I got Jell-O shots for the ride, but I gotta see some ID. I'm no idiot. Hey, what do they call you guys, 2 Chainz?" Carol kept laughing but Ava and Eva didn't get the joke. I told them it was because they were wearing tacky belly chains, but they still didn't get it. I don't wanna talk sh*t about my friends, but they're, like, really dumb sometimes.

Anyways, we got into the back of the car and it was lined with velvet and loud music was playing and Carol kept screaming about how much she loved Stephen Wolf's "Magic Carpet Ride" or something. And then all of a sudden it smelled like rotten lasagna and the inside of a butthole and Eva yelled "GODDAMMIT, AVA!" And Ava said it wasn't her and Carol told us it was probably Mr. Todd, the potbellied pig that was lying on a white bedsheet in the very back of the car. He looked super dead, but then he breathed and it was gross, but I also thought it was kind of cool to have a pig in the car. Like, very anti-Pinterest.

Carol checked our IDs and handed us Jell-O shots and told us that when Mr. Todd eats too much Chipotle he farts so hard. She actually gave us a second shot because she felt bad that the car smelled like so much sh*t. Then she slammed on the gas and drove onto the road like a total badass. The twins and I did our secret cheers and took another shot and the shots were, like, SO GOOD. Carol told us the secret was a little bit of basil at the very end to give it a fresh kick. She told us she learned that from the Food Network host with the "big ol' breasts." At this point, I was like totally loving Carol.

We were in the middle of our second round of secret cheers (and I seriously can't tell you how to do it because it's a Sigma secret), but then a group of Pi Kappa boys on glider boards glided into the street. No offense, but they looked like a bunch of idiots. Carol swerved and we screamed and all three RED Jell-O shots LANDED IN MY CROTCH. I screamed, "OH MY GOD!" and the twins screamed, "OH MY GOD," and then Carol pulled the car over and got out screaming, "I'm not letting a buncha dumb-asses on dumb-ass George Jetson skateboards ruin my star rating." Then she took a baseball bat and Mr. Todd and walked over to the Pi Kappas. Seriously, Carol and Mr. Todd are squad goals.

Anyways, Eva and Ava tried to help, but they both forgot their stain sticks and now they're furiously reapplying lip gloss to each

other, which is their version of a panic attack, so they're useless. So dumb! Now we're like five or so minutes away from the party, and instead of Snapchatting this, I decided to write you this, like, unnecessarily overdetailed email asking for help. I've got red stains all over the crotchular region of my H&M white pants, what do I do?! On the bright side, it smells great but it still definitely looks like I'm period-ing all over myself. HELP.

Sincerely,
**Blotch on the Crotch
from Dover, Delaware**

Dear Blotch on the Crotch,

Sounds like you're in the middle of a Code Red. Do not despair. As long as you have red spots on the crotch of your pants and not on your crotch itself, you're doing okay. Here's what I think your options are...

You could, **one**, **ask for help**. Since the twins are out of commission, it leaves you with ride-or-die Carol and Mr. Todd. You could ask Carol if she has any soda water; that's supposed to get out stains. But judging by the sound of Carol, I have a feeling the only liquid in her car is gonna be some Fanta and some antifreeze. But what about Mr. Todd's white sheet? Carol seems like an off-kilter maternal type and obviously cares about maintaining her unexpectedly impeccable Uber rating, so she's got to let you take it. And if she does, you just have to decide: sarong or toga? In most scenarios, you'd probably opt for the sarong, but you're in *college*. College is to a toga like a buffet is to an elastic waistband.

The only thing you'll have to worry about is the presumably awful scent. Why not see if Carol's got any of that fresh basil she loves in the glove compartment? If so, rub that all over yourself; no one can deny the fresh scent of basil (the Food Network chef with the "big ol' breasts" agrees). And worst-case scenario, Spacey's house will probably smell like a barn anyway. Also don't forget about Ava's potentially terrible toots stealing scent focus.

You could, **two**, **creatively convert**. One way to creatively convert is the toga route. But if for some reason the sheet has some unforeseen mystery stains, or Mr. Todd has some deep-seated psychological attachment to it, you'll have to think of other options. The easy options are: Will your shirt cover it? Is your shirt big enough that you could lose the pants altogether and rock a T-shirt dress like an Olsen twin? Can you place a shoulder bag in front of it like the way they hide a pregnant actress on a sitcom? If the stains haven't gone all the way through, you can possibly turn the pants inside out and pretend to be the quirky girl at the party who LOVES *Back to the Future*. If that doesn't work, try cutting or ripping the jeans into shorts and tie the cut-off pant legs around your waist like a chunky belt or unique design element. If anyone asks, tell them your cousin is a student at the Fashion Institute and made them for you. Kids in Delaware will eat that sh*t up.

You could, **three**, **alter the scenario**. Time for a drive-by DIY! Snag a couple more of Carol's delectable Jell-O concoctions and smear them on your shirt to make it look like blood coming out of a gunshot wound on your side. Dab a couple other spots around the original crotch stains and continue down one of your legs. Use your eyeliner pencil to draw on a goatee and borrow the first pair of fake hipster glasses you see at the party (trust me, there will be some), and voilà, you're WALTER WHITE. This getup not only conceals the stains, but also helps weed out the dum-dum partygoers from the ones who actually have a sense of humor AND will most likely win the favor of great-jawline-disproportionate-calfed party host Kevin Spacey. Also bonus points to you if you can snag a fedora/top hat hybrid off of one of the douchey frat boys to complete the look. If you don't want to go that far (bummer!), try dabbing the Jell-O shots down the rest of your pant legs and call it tie-dye. Tie-dye is very trendy, says the Internet.

You could, **four**, **own it**. So, you stained your pants. It's a *white* party. You're probably in the minority if you end the night without ruining your outfit. Granted, red isn't the optimum color of stain you'd hope for, but you're also in a station wagon with a potbellied pig named Mr. Todd, so no time to fuss over the details.

Here are some go-to red-carpet poses.

You embrace those stains and walk into the party with confidence. If anyone asks you about your appearance, tell them you got "Jell-O shot" and that it's a new game some college out west invented that's sort of like that game Assassin. You have to try to "assassinate" other people at the party by marking them with a Jell-O shot without getting noticed, and the last person standing without a Jell-O–shot stain wins. If you get assassinated you have to drink the Jell-O shot that killed you. College kids LOVE drinking games and LOVE touching each other; they won't be able to resist this game. Now look at you: you just created the most popular party game since beer pong. Well, technically, I did. But I'll let you have it. You've been through a lot.

Also, no matter what happens, you met Carol tonight. And that's worth celebrating.

Hope this wasn't the worst advice in the whole goddamn world.

Sincerely,
Miss Mess

"I wear my sort of clothes to save me the trouble of deciding which clothes to wear."
—KATHARINE HEPBURN

"I wear my sort of clothes to save me the trouble of having to run out outside naked if my house catches on fire in the middle of the night."
—GRACE HELBIG

Dear Miss Mess,

I was trying to decide between the eggplant Parmesan and the mussels by imagining which dish looked less awkward to eat. I didn't want to repeat what happened a month ago with the veterinarian at the Mexican place. No one tells you how difficult tacos are to eat on a date. Woof. But the past is in the past; and the vet said the salsa didn't burn his eyes *too* much. Besides, this date was already going better than the last anyway.

Marc, my date, actually looks like his profile picture ᴀɴᴅ he really does own the dog in it and didn't just borrow one to seem relatable. And my doubts about him being stupid because he spells his name with a *c* were fading. Plus I'm wearing that brand-new black jumpsuit that makes me look like an adorable janitor with the black pumps that make me look like a *sexy* adorable janitor. The kind of janitor you'd find at one of those spicy Upper East Side prep schools in a CW show. To me this outfit says, *I want you to find my personality more interesting than my boobs. And if you do, I'll likely show you my boobs.*

I was feeling confident all around.

Marc told me to stay away from the eggplant Parm because the last time he had it he "didn't leave [his] toilet for a week." Which was kinda weird and made me wonder why he'd bring a date to a place where he got food poisoning. I started thinking maybe this wasn't a date but an elaborate plot to kidnap me. But my therapist told me this week that I need to stop watching those *Taken* movies because if I keep assuming that everyone is trying to kidnap me, I won't have any sustainable relationships.

So I laughed it off and told Marc that the same thing happened to me with falafel a couple weeks ago. And then I realized that this had never happened and that I was doing my lying thing again. My therapist also said if I keep making up stories to make other people feel comfortable, I won't be able to build a solid relationship foundation with anyone. But before I could continue my lie, the waiter dropped off two glasses of wine and asked what we'd like to eat.

In a panic, I ordered some Italian thing that was the first thing I saw on the menu that *wasn't* the eggplant Parm. Marc ordered spaghetti and meatballs. Which made me forget all about him having explosive diarrhea for a second because I started to get really turned on by the overall simplicity of this guy. We clinked our wineglasses and I accidentally drank almost the whole glass of Chardonnay before realizing it. But when I put my glass down, I saw that almost all of his wine was gone in one swig, too, and both of us started cracking up.

He made a joke about being a functional alcoholic and I stopped laughing because I couldn't tell if he was serious or not. But then he told me he was just kidding and I mostly believed him because he looks just like Paul Rudd at the end of *Clueless* when he's all clean and in a suit and humbled by falling in love with someone he never thought he'd be attracted to. I started to ask Marc a question but then instantly forgot what I was going to say and ended up asking him what his dog ate. Like an IDIOT.

But before he could answer, a bell rang and Dean Martin's "That's Amore" started to play. All of the serving staff, along with the hosts and some kitchen crew, assembled in the dining area. They raised their glasses and sang while pulling people from their tables to dance around the room with them. A much older cook with the name tag "Tony," who was *very obviously* missing his two front teeth, grabbed me and pulled me into the routine. I looked at Marc to save me, but instead he just handed me my wineglass with a goddamn adorable smile. I tried to hide my panic as best I could. I was not bred for dancing. I was bred for enjoying complimentary bread while other people danced. We shuffled in and out of tables clinking glasses with everyone we passed, yelling, "...when the moon hits your eye!"

We shuffled past the hostess stand and my heel snagged a divot in the marble floor. Toothless Tony urged me forward and I felt my shoe snap and release and I immediately realized the heel of my sexy pump had popped off. Tony kept singing into my ear and it smelled like cigars and anchovies. The song ended and the dining room applauded while I finally got back to my table and attempted to sit like both of my feet existed at equal heights.

Marc complimented me and we made some jokes about Tony until I excused myself to go to the bathroom to figure out my mess. When I walked in there, an adorable old Italian woman working as the bathroom attendant with a name tag that read "Martha" greeted me. She smelled like pepperoni and roses. I was going to ask her for help but she didn't seem to speak any English. Instead, I've been curled up in this stall writing this excessively long and comprehensive email to you, hoping that Marc doesn't think my bowels are exploding from some sort of wine poisoning. My digestive system is balanced, but my heels are not. What should I do?

Sincerely,
Ghetto Stiletto
in Denver, Colorado

Dear Ghetto Stiletto,

Is Tony single? Just kidding. But if he's got a full-toothed grandson, send him my way. They sound like fun people. Back to the point. No need to worry. Just *pump* the breaks and listen. Let's see what we can do here.

You could, **one**, **ask for help.** In a desperate panic you could opt to ask Martha (using a crude version of charades) or another random person in the bathroom for spare shoes and/or to switch shoes with you. Approach it like a fun adult-lady sorority game. I've never been in a sorority but I imagine it's 70 percent creative shoe swapping, 10 percent posing for and posting Instagram pictures, 10 percent parties with fruit-infused punches, and 10 percent group crying. Who knows, you might get lucky and come across someone completely secure in their long-term relationship who has a shoe size identical to yours and nothing to lose who might agree to switch with you. Or in a long shot you could phone the nearest friend to make a discreet shoe drop at the hostess stand. There should be an Uber for remote wardrobe malfunctions. Any Silicon Valley tech heads down to develop this? I'll give you one percent off the back end and one group cry.

You could, **two**, **creatively convert.** Is it possible to break the heel of your other shoe to match the already broken one? If so, hopefully your date won't notice you went from sexy pumps to flats that look like dogs made them. But at least they match. If you can't break the heel of the other shoe, is there a way to pull your pant leg down to cover the back of the shoe and leave the David-Blaine-levitating illusion of a heel? Just make sure your date never walks behind you.

I doubt you'd let him walk behind you anyway on account of your constant abduction delusions.

You could, **three**, **alter the scenario**. This isn't the best option in this instance. It seems like you tend to alter your reality enough as it is, so let's avoid this route.

You could, **four**, **own it**. You broke your shoe! So what! You broke it dancing with a toothless old man in an Italian restaurant . . . What a story! Walk back to your Paul-Rudd-on-a-good-day wannabe and tell him it turns out Tony *actually* swept you off your feet. And when you both get done groaning at how cheesy that sounded, hopefully you can share a laugh, in between furiously making out because this heel-break scenario shines a light on the fact that you're both kinda crazy, attractive people with a sense of humor, which is truly the only way to be on account of the fact that we're all going to die someday and finding someone as bonkers as you with optimism and a silly sensibility is IMPOSSIBLE on Tinder, so you both seize the moment and find a twenty-four-hour wedding chapel and . . . eat gelato across the street from it because THANK GOD it was closed for fumigation.

Hope this wasn't the worst advice in the whole goddamn world.

Sincerely,
Miss Mess

"Style is a simple way of saying complicated things." —JEAN COCTEAU

"Style is a simple way of saying I showered." —GRACE HELBIG

grace expectations

WHAT DOES YOUR DENIM SAY ABOUT YOU?

Skinny Jeans mean you're hip, you're cool, you're fashion forward, and you're full of guacamole and self-doubt. You won't ever encourage people to look at your butt, but you won't stop them from sneaking some peeking. You like margaritas (no salt on the rim even though you reaLLy want salt on the rim) and your Tinder profile says you like "good times with great company" and hikes. But the last time you hiked, you walked for five minutes, took an Instagram photo, and left to find a decent manicure and a Mexican place with a happy hour.

You're an avid Pinterester and you can't resist a good brunch or over-adjective'd Starbucks order. You care about issues and charities but it's really hard to balance getting involved when Zara is having its end-of-season sale. (Let the record state, I wear these jeans all the time, and yes, I am very full of guacamole.)

Bootcut Jeans are like the Southwest egg rolls to your mozzarella sticks: they're slightly more exotic but still a safe choice. If you opt for bootcut jeans, I assume you're a new mom in your midthirties from Maryland out on the town for the first Friday night since your chest domes ceased lactating. That or you're a lady who works on a farm and actually needs the slightly wider cuff to accommodate the boots you wear strictly for work and not fashion purposes. Either way, you spend most of your day tossing a bunch of slop into the mouths of some underdeveloped animals.

Flared Jeans mean…well, I don't know that anyone who wears flared jeans would actually buy this book. There are a lot of wind chimes and crystals to be bought first. And don't think I'm being mean. I went to Sedona once and left with $100 worth of amethyst crystals because a lady told me they "could" calm anxiety. That said, here's a business proposition for anyone interested: Amethyst-Crystal-Crotch-Lined Lady JNCOs. THINK ABOUT IT!

Straight Jeans mean you're gay. That or you're very good at the intellectual career you've chosen for yourself and devote more time to that endeavor than attempting to understand or experiment with fashion. Good for you.

Boyfriend Jeans mean you either just broke up with your boyfriend, you're bloated, you paint houses for a living, you're a toddler, or you recently lost a lot of weight and now your old skinny jeans look like boyfriend jeans.

Jorts (aka jean shorts) mean your ankles got hot and why would you go shopping when you have scissors? Besides, you're too busy listening to Limp Bizkit and trying to find your moccasins to go buy "real" shorts. And the rest of your day is full of Xbox, Xtube, getting high, and Miller High Life. You were a philosophy major for a second, and now you're a student of life. When people question you about your lifestyle, you point to your "think outside the bun" tramp stamp and shrug your shoulders. You're a sloppy, floppy paradox.

"Fashion is not necessarily about labels. It's not about brands. It's about something else that comes from within you."
—RALPH LAUREN ·

"Fashion is not necessarily about labels. It's not about brands. It's about that hungover depression that comes from within you that motivates you to spend $300 on gap.com."
—GRACE HELBIG

Just because the forecast calls for cloudy weather doesn't mean you can't dress like sunshine.

street style

GPS: GRACE PRETENDS STREETS (ARE REAL PEOPLE)

I'm sure you've heard of the term "street style" before.

A lot of designers take inspiration from the streets because . . . well, they're the birthplace of trends and the breeding ground of fashion. If you're unfamiliar, fear not, I've been on many different streets over the years, so allow me to break it down for you.

Avenues are very chic. They have a classic elegance and usually lead to something luxurious. They're dramatic and can take up a lot of space with their grandiose presence. They're timeless, beautiful, and attract a lot of old people. They're very Barneys meets Saks. And they hang with Bloomingdale's but they talk about her behind her back.

Highways are all business. They're smooth, sleek, industrial, and very monochromatic. They prefer to blend in. They're practical and predictable and can be just plain boring. It's really hard to party with a highway. They're very Ann Taylor meets RadioShack.

Dirt Roads are free spirits. They're wild, unkempt, and usually have a lot of holes. They attract a wide variety of people, from young tripping college types to old hairless hillbillies. You never know what you're gonna get with a dirt road. They might lead you to the greatest party; they might lead you to the most terrifying murder cabin. It's always a gamble with them, but a memorable one. Because no matter what they show you, you usually wake up with a sore butt the next day. They're Wet Seal meets REI meets Boot Barn.

Cul-de-sacs and Courts scream suburban sophisticated. They play it safe with their style; they keep everything tucked in. They're family-friendly, relatively uniform, and tend to have an underlying superiority complex. They don't consider themselves Ross Dress for Less, they're Marshalls. They're not Payless Shoe Source, they're DSW. They're not JCPenney's, they're Macy's.

Alleys are edgy. They're darker and less obvious. They're stereotypically associated with drug deals and wizards. They usually have an air of "city cool" mixed with a gritty artistic aesthetic. They're rough around the edges in a culturally stylish way. They're Urban Outfitters meets Rag & Bone meets a cigar shop.

Saturday, Sept. 26, 2015

Dear Diary,

I don't even know where to begin. So much has happened. I've officially been at the MOA for one whole day and it's been straight-up bonkers. It's taking a lot more getting used to than I thought it would. And trust me, I've been bursting at the seams to tell you all about it, but I've just been too tied up. Sorry, Diary, I'm reusing puns already, I'M ALL OVER THE PLACE.

So, my big day had come: I was about to head to the MOA. I sat in the kitchen next to the window with my duffel bags packed, checking through the curtains every three seconds thinking I heard my ride. My SweatMom and SweatDad shuffled over to say good-bye. They began to get a little choked up, but then a new episode of *Judge Judy* started playing on the TV, so they quickly said their sloppy good-byes and sank back into their beanbag chairs. Suddenly I heard a horn from outside and the knots in my stomach jumped. I looked out the window and saw a shiny white truck with the word "FedEx" beautifully written on the sides. It was just like the commercial.

Just then my G-Wind wandered out from the back room holding a shoe box. She handed it to me, and when I asked her what was inside, she said, "I can't tell you just yet. But you'll know the right time to open it." I looked at her confused and she said, "Okay, yes, I got stoned and watched a lot of *Harry Potter* last night. Regardless, this box is very special to me, so take good care of it. Try not to open it until you get there."

I shoved the box as carefully as possible into one of my bags and headed for the truck.

A man lifted open the back door and in front of me was an amazing, tarnished, silver-lined interior with beautifully shabby shelves and scraps of aged, stained cardboard strewn around. It was magical. There were already a bunch of other clothes on the shelves talking and laughing and throwing old mailing labels at each other. I hopped in and tried to sit in an open seat next to a pair of Nike running shoes, but she looked me up and down and told me the seat was saved for yoga pants. So instead, I found a spot next to a pair of Birkenstocks. "Ugh, don't even waste your time with the athletic wear," Birkenstock said. "But I'm athletic wear, too, I just thought—" Before I could finish the sentence, Nike running shoes cut me off and said "Correction, you're *pathetic* wear." All the other clothes started laughing until

Birkenstock chimed in and said, "No, what's *actually* pathetic is how cheap it is to make you and how expensive your price point is." A bunch of "ooohs" swept the shelves and the Nike tightened her laces and turned around to continue talking to neon-pink Lululemon yoga pants.

I couldn't believe Birkenstock stood up for me like that. She didn't even know me. I thanked her and she told me to call her "Birk." I told her she could call me "Sweat" because I panicked and couldn't think of any other nickname. We ended up talking the rest of the way there. She's a sophomore, so she already survived the freshman grind. She told me a bunch of her horror stories. Like how all the upper-class Jimmy Choos haze the incoming shoe freshmen by dousing them with Odor-Eaters while the Vans sneakers draw all over them with permanent marker. And getting permanent marker out of suede is apparently impossible. Another time, last winter, a group of the Victoria's Secret bras got drunk on Love Spell Body Mist and threw a bunch of freshmen into the freezers at Benihana because it's tradition for the bras to throw anyone they can into a freezer. Ironic, I guess?

"You're really putting me at ease," I told her, and she replied, "Yeah, when it comes to presenting the bright side of things, I can't say I'm very persuasive." I laughed and told her I got the joke.

She looked at me confused, and I said, "Per-SUEDE-sive?... Suede?"

"Oh. I wasn't meaning to make a joke," she said. There was an awkward silence. "But freshman year is pretty tricky, so if I were you, I'd *buckle* up," she said, pointing to her buckle. We both laughed like dorks and kept making dumb puns until we finally arrived at the MOA.

The back door lifted and it was an immediate free-for-all. Over the calamity of everyone grabbing their things, I could see it: a huge concrete building, surrounded by a sea of shipping trucks with clothing and accessories pouring out of each one. It was a playground of activity. Trouser pants pushed past me, evening gowns elbowed their way in, blazers were halting halter tops while fingerless gloves flirted with scarves and skirts screamed at jorts. How was I ever going to find Dr. Scholls in all of this? I grabbed my things and started to make my way toward any entrance I could find. I kept getting jostled around until I heard Birk's voice yelling "Hey, Sweat! Sweatpants! Over here!"

I made my way over and found her standing with a pair of overalls. And those overalls were RIPPED, Diary. Allow me to be more specific: he was tattered and shredded in all the right places with a perfectly faded wash and brass hardware. I didn't realize I was staring at him so hard until Birk kicked me in the knee. "Sweat, this is Rees, he's a fellow sophomore. Rees, this is Sweat, she's a freshman."

"Rees?" I questioned.

"It's short for Dungarees. It's a family name." God, he was so cool.

"Cool, yeah, Sweat is short for S-Sweatpants," I stuttered like an IDIOT.

"Yeah, I figured."

I froze. *Duh. He's not an idiot like you are.* I couldn't think of anything to say, I was so

Grace's sweatpants from Topshop

lost in his stitches. Just then a man's voice came up, yelling, "Sweatpants! There you are!" It was Dr. Scholls. He introduced himself and gave me a huge hug. Sweet but SO embarrassing.

"Hi, Dr. Scholls," Birk said.

"Oh, hello, Birk; hello, Rees. How were your summers?"

"Really great. I actually ended up doing the study abroad you recommended. The one in India," Rees replied. INDIA?! OMG, HE'S SO COOL.

"Sweat, we're gonna go find our storage containers; we'll catch you later," Birk said. She and Rees walked off and I couldn't stop watching Rees's back pockets until Dr. Scholls finally snapped me out of it.

"Let's get you inside and settled. How was your ride?"

As I told him about my travels to get to the MOA, we made our way into the giant structure and I was immediately overwhelmed. The floors were so shiny, the stores were so bright, the music was so generic, and I was in heaven! Dr. Scholls walked me to the information desk, where we got in the longest line I'd ever seen in my life. "It moves quicker than it looks. We just need to pick up your registration," he said. While we waited we talked about what classes I was most excited about and what supplies I should make sure to pick up. Dr. Scholls had a very delicate way about him; you could tell he was an old sole. Just as we were getting onto the topic of G-Wind, a pair of reading glasses behind the desk interrupted, asking for my name. That line did move fast!

"Sweatpants," I told him.

He gave me a look, and after searching through his iPad, he said, "Not here."

"Actually, I think it's under 'Scholls,'" the doctor replied, giving me a wink. I totally forgot! I'm here as Dr. Scholls's granddaughter twice restocked. I'm in disguise. Thinking that made me feel so cool. But then I felt like a dork for feeling cool about it.

"You're in the North Garden," Glasses said, and handed me a welcome packet. "That's this way, dear, toward Nordstrom." Dr. Scholls started to lead me toward a long hallway when two identical sharp suits stepped into our path. "Is this her, Scholls, the granddaughter twice restocked?" one of the suits questioned.

Dr. Scholls seemed caught off guard. "Uh, yes, this is her. Dear, I'd like you to meet the superintendents of the MOA, the Brooks Brothers." It was them. The men that banned my G-Wind all those years ago. I could understand immediately why G-Wind would hate these guys. They were too pressed, too fitted, too stiff. They looked like two money-laundering bank managers.

A swell of anger rose in me and I blurted out, "You guys look way too young to be the Brooks Brothers." Dr. Scholls was shocked. "No offense," I added.

"Well, dear, that's, uh, maybe not—"

"Oh, don't worry, Scholls, it's okay. We get that all the time. We've had a lot of tailoring, dear," one of them said to me with a slim smile. "We're very happy to have you joining us this year; your essays were quite impressive. It seems that intelligence must run in the *family*." As he said that he looked at Dr. Scholls, who was avoiding eye contact.

"Scholls, can we chat with you a moment?" the other superintendent asked.

"I'm sorry, would you excuse me?" Dr. Scholls said. "Will you be okay going to the North Garden without me? It's just up there—if you pass the Claire's, you've gone too far. But if you see Claire, tell her I said hello and that I'm still finding time to check out her new collection of septum rings, I haven't forgotten." I nodded and made sure to give the superintendents my most suspicious look before heading off down the hallway.

I got to my storage container right by the Sunglass Hut and started to unpack my things and map out my schedule for the week on the personal directory they gave me. This place is MASSIVE, Diary, and right as I was about to give up on getting anywhere on time, Birk and Rees stopped by and asked me if I wanted to grab some sushi. I tried to shove all my embarrassing stain sticks and extra waist cords under my shelves. "Oh God, did the Abercrombie & Fitch polos already send you a piss missile?" Rees said, walking over to the shoe box my G-Wind gave me before I left.

"NO!" I screamed, grabbing the box. Rees was so confused. "Uh, no, sorry, this is from home, actually. Just some personal stuff," I said, trying to play it cool.

"Very cool," Rees replied. "Homesickness is pretty common freshman year; you're smart to plan ahead." HE SAID I WAS SMART.

Over sushi, Birk and Rees filled me in on more of the important things I needed to know about the MOA. The kind of stuff they don't print in the brochures. Like, that a piss missile is a prank the A&F polos pull on the freshmen by sending them anonymous shoe boxes of A&F boxers covered in piss and A&F cologne. You, and everything around you when you open the box, end up smelling awful for days. They also told me their conspiracy theory about the food at Chipotle being made with mind-control drugs since EVERYONE eats there constantly. We talked for a while about our families; Birk's parents were students here and now teach underprivileged shoes at an outlet mall outside of Portland. Rees, on the other hand, was adopted by a well-to-do denim family. "I'm Lucky Brand," he said.

"I may as well be adopted. I mean, I'm technically enrolled here in disguise," I started to tell them.

"What do you mean?" Rees asked.

"Do you guys know about Black Friday?" They both looked at me like I dropped Kool-Aid on a pair of white pants. Before I could explain anything, a voice announced over the PA system, "Attention, students, the MOA will be closing in ten minutes, please return to your storage containers for the night."

Suddenly we were being hustled out of the food court by a bunch of suits. Birk and Rees looked at me, and Rees said, "We need to continue this conversation later!" When I got back to my storage container, I saw the shoe box my G-Wind left me sitting under a shelf.

I reached out to open it, and as soon as I tried to get the lid off, the voice of my G-Wind started up, saying "SweatG! It's G-Wind! Is this working? Can you hear me? If you can hear me, then scoodily-doo! It wasn't a waste of fifty dollars! I knew you'd try to open this thing before the right time, so I looked up this voice security system to freak you out. Are you freaked out? Good! I told you to wait to open this thing and you didn't. But I understand. You're probably overwhelmed right now. The MOA is a lot to take in. But you're my SweatG, so I know you can handle it. Remember, even the shiniest floors get walked on. Does that make sense? Anyshoes, don't try to open this until the right time, young ladypants. Okay? Okay. I love you, darling! Buh-bye! Don't sweat the small stuff, that's what I should have said, goddammit! Is this thing still recording? If it is, don't sweat the small stuff, SweatG! Forget everything else I said! Love you!" And then there were three extra minutes of my G-Wind fumbling around because apparently she didn't know how to turn off the recording.

I passed out right after it finished; I didn't realize how tired I was. And now here I am the next morning, scrambling to fill you in on everything before I have to run to my first class. You couldn't hear it, Diary, because you're a Diary, but an Elton John song just started up over the PA system, which means we have five minutes to get to our first class. I'll write in you again soon!

Love,
Sweatpants

Grace

hair...makeup...accessories

hair...makeup

The art of manifest accessory...The art of arranging human boo

The art of distracting others from the real mess................

The art of convincing people you didn't get bangs because you're sa

The art of "Is this too much?"...........

The art of decorating your Christmas tree carcass...........

accessories

row pillows"...The art of brushing, blushing, and rushing............

.........The art of tools, jewels, and regretting bangs...

........The art of dyeing so you don't think about dying......

The art of dyeing, applying, and trying too hard.......

The art of making yourself louder without saying anything...

vintage grace

I WAS THE DAUGHTER OF AN AVON LADY

My relationship with makeup started at a young age, against my will.

You might not know this, but I come from a dark, contoured past. When I was growing up, my family was in the makeup drug-mule business.

My mother was an Avon lady.

For those of you who don't know what that is, let me paint you a delightfully desperate picture. Imagine those Girl Scouts who hawk cookies outside the local grocery store. They blindly exploit themselves and their delicious wares for the sake of a larger entity, under the guise that if they sell the most boxes, they can win that Barbie bike that Barbie herself definitely never rode on account of it messing up her hair, but still... a BARBIE BIKE.

Now imagine those same girls as forty-year-old women. But instead of cookies, they're selling inexpensive makeup with the same blind ambition as their eleven-year-old predecessors. But they're not competing for a Barbie bike; instead they're competing to convince their clients they can look like Barbie.

OOF.

But everyone's gotta make a living. My well-intentioned mother spent a few years of my childhood moonlighting (during the early afternoons) as an Avon lady while balancing single motherhood and real-world-job-hood in an attempt to support three beautiful ~~monsters~~ children.

Maybe she was born that way? Maybe she selflessly worked her butt off to create a cool life for her kids?

As a little girl, I had no awareness of what was going on; only in my adult years have I had time to reflect and understand that the life of an Avon lady has a LOT of hilarious parallels to drug smuggling.

The life of an Avon lady has a lot of hilarious parallels to drug smuggling.

Like a real drug lord (or at least like the ones movies tell me about), my wonderful-and-will-hate-me-forever-for-ever-comparing-her-Avon-ladying-to-selling-drugs mother had small plastic bags of travel-sized makeup samples all over her dresser. She had messy stacks of envelopes for monthly orders and suspicious-looking-powder-smudged makeup mirrors from her translucent powders and loose eye shadow.

My mom was a South Jersey makeup *boss*.

I have no idea how much makeup she actually sold on a weekly/biweekly/monthly basis, but I do know that every other week we drove to an ambiguous and kinda grimy apartment complex where she'd draft me or my older brother to run an envelope up to a mysterious apartment. We never questioned it. She'd tell us to put the envelope under the door, knock quickly, and hurry back to the

Grace & her younger brother

car. Never questioned a single second of it; I was too distracted by my own stupid puberty, and my older brother was neck-deep in his Magic: The Gathering decks.

It wasn't until I saw *Requiem for a Dream* in college that I noticed the similarities between my mom's Avon transactions and the drug trade and thought, *Well, thank God Avon never made any double-ended lip glosses. That could have been real bad.*

I've had a curious relationship with makeup. As I was growing up, my mom's room was always full of new face paints and powders and pencils. She accumulated an extensive makeup collection mainly because she was a passive salesperson and had to meet an Avon quota each month, so she'd end up buying herself different products in order to skate by. From time to time I'd watch her put on makeup while she openly admitted that she had no idea what she was doing. Usually she'd get distracted by something else she had to do for us and would settle for however her eyeliner looked in one take. And almost every time it was a good half inch above her eyeline. God bless.

I learned a lot about makeup (intentionally and unintentionally) from my mom. I also learned a lot from magazines, makeover shows, and from one of the most formative makeup moments of my life, my senior-prom makeover.

My high school prom was a solid four out of ten. And the prep process was a solid "ehhh" out of "awww." I didn't have a ton of girl-friends in high school, but I still wanted to feel "young, fun, and independent" while I got ready for what magazines told me was my "big night." So my mom gave me some money to get my hair done at the JCPenney's hair salon—yes, JCPenney has a hair salon, and yes, it lives up to the "penneys" name. They specialize in creating styles that look great from far away done by women who refuse to under-stand if you don't like something. To us, it was luxury; it wasn't a Supercuts, it was a *salon.* My mom got her hair dyed there from time to time (when she'd consolidate her coupons like a TLC reality show and get a dye job for the price of a single pair of panties). I'd go with her, thinking she was a suburban Mariah Carey; we'd spend the day at the salon getting pampered (i.e., she'd be put under a dryer next to some dying daffodils and a giant print of a woman with a razor-sharp bob while I read *Seventeen* magazines from six months earlier).

To get my prom hair done at Penney's was a treat. My mom defi-nitely didn't have money for that, but somehow she made sure it happened. God bless that lovely lady. It was 2003 and messy asym-metrical updos were all the rage. But I knew when I asked my forty-plus-year-old Penney's stylist for a "choppy updo" that I was in for a surprise. And I was surprised . . . that she was able to give me some-thing close to what I wanted! It was definitely piece-y and choppy and 2,394,723,765,239 other stylists in the salon made sure to give me compliments as if to force me into feeling like it was exactly what I asked for. Good enough for me! Success!

I had been getting my hair dyed, cut, colored, and permed (OOF) for years.

Now on to the makeup part.

I had been getting my hair dyed, cut, colored, and permed (OOF) for years, so the concept of having my hair professionally done wasn't an entirely new feeling. It definitely wasn't familiar, but it was way more familiar than GETTING MY MAKEUP DONE! Which was what every girl did for prom. Makeup separated the babies from the babes. It wasn't prom unless a professional was putting things on your face. My mom not only gave me money to get my hair done at Penney's, but she also gave me some cash and the suggestion of walking across the mall to the Macy's makeup counter to get my makeup done. The women at those counters will give you an entire makeover if you promise to buy at least one product from them. It was something I'd never done before and would never think of doing now, but the adrenaline rush of grooming and graduating took hold of me and I walked right up and asked a lady with an aggressive amount of various products on her face if I could get my makeup done for prom. She and her coworkers immediately "aww'd" and I immediately got awkward. I felt so out of place in comparison to their exaggerated eyebrows and pronounced pouts.

When she asked what I was wearing, I told her a black halter dress, and this lit up her life. A black dress was a blank slate. With a "fun updo" already in place, her creativity knew no bounds. Every color/product/look she suggested I blindly agreed to. She was swiping iridescent colors on my eyelids and wiping highlighters on my cheeks. I felt like Tai in the makeover montage from *Clueless*.

But the results weren't exactly the same. When she finished her last swish of mascara, just like at the salon, the other makeup artists started aggressively complimenting the makeup artist and me on my new look. All of them had such extravagantly contoured expressions—if they thought I looked good, I thought that I must look like a member of the Insane Clown Posse. My makeup artist offered me a handheld mirror, and I looked... *fine?* ah! no! I looked like a lady of the night in training. My eyelids were silver-coated disco balls twirling above a mouth overrun with dark lip liner and frosted lipstick. I was ready to apply for my new life as the failed sixth Spice Girl. And it wasn't the makeup artist's fault. To her credit she gave me a look that I didn't say no to. Ironically, I think I ended up buying the silver eye shadow to pay for the transformation. I quickly said thank you while the other makeup artists were still gushing over my eyes, and rushed to my car.

When I got home, I lost it. I ran into the bathroom and started crying. My mom immediately came to comfort me, agreeing that yeah, my eyes looked kind of crazy. The worst part was that the hair and makeup had taken so much time that my date was already on his way. (I went to my senior prom with a friend from my track team. He was handsome and nice and quiet. We had a minor moment of infatuation, but it was very bland after that.)

But I wasn't worried about what I looked like for him (no offense, Jake!), I was more concerned about living up to the magazine-mandated standards that had been pushed onto my person. According to my superficial calculations, I was currently failing at my perfect prom appearance. So, with minutes to spare, my mom and I MacGyver'd bits and pieces of her Avon makeup in an attempt to soften my unintentionally eighties-inspired look. We ended up with something I can say I don't hate and am not completely embarrassed by. It was very 2003. In fact, it was so striking that my teachers voted me into prom court. (My school did a really PC thing my senior year: they allowed two girls and two guys to get chosen to prom court by student vote and three to get chosen by teacher vote from the runway show before the actual prom. Before the dance, everyone (who wanted to) participated in a runway show in the auditorium of our high school. It's where they took the classic prom photos every year, but to make it more "fun," they added the runway portion, where three teachers would choose three guys and three girls who they thought "looked great" to make it onto prom court. Very *American Idol*. From there, the five girls and five guys opened a box with a rose inside. If you got the red rose, you were crowned King or Queen. It was the school's way of trying to prove Prom King and Queen wasn't just a popularity contest. It was also a gambling and looks contest judged by slightly bitter teachers who had nothing better to do on a Saturday night. Fun!)

But somehow my choppy, sloppy, overly sultry look won the respect of the teachers and I made it onto prom court. I did not win

Prom Queen, thank God. I don't think my brain could've handled any more unexpected attention that day. Instead, I celebrated my loss by awkwardly slow-dancing with my white rose and my quiet date.

My fascination with makeup has grown and evolved. In high school, I'd watch all kinds of makeover shows on TV. My dad used to take me and my brothers to the bookstore pretty regularly and I'd stand in the magazine section trying to absorb all the *Seventeen* and *YM* articles about "which glitter shadow is this fall's go-to" as fast as I could so I wouldn't have to actually buy the magazine. I did, though, buy a Bobbi Brown makeup guidebook in high school. And now I currently binge on YouTube beauty guru videos whenever I'm hungover or feeling generally disgusting.

I really like makeup. I think it's fun. It can make you feel a lot of things: confident, sexy, cute, gothic, glamorous, etc. Look how powerful it made those guys in KISS feel.

basics

MAKEUP

Obviously, I'm no master makeup artist.

Though I've attempted to "paint the barn" on my own, I've also had enough pretty professionals take a brush to my face to give me an understanding of the basics.

I have to admit it feels a little self-serving to take up readers' time talking about what I like and use and blah blah blah. But then I remember that I genuinely enjoy hearing about the things other people are into because it educates me about new products and techniques. It's how I learned that filling in your eyebrows is a thing. So, without further uncertain adieu, here are the essential members of my makeup bag.

Sidenote: The specific products I use change constantly because new makeup is created faster than new potato chip flavors (how old am I?!). Also I buy a lot of my makeup like a kid who gets three minutes in a toy store to pick out as many things as she wants. I tend to just grab stuff without thinking until I'm out of time.

Moisturizer: I don't use it nearly as often as I should. It's like dental floss for the face. I buy it with the best intentions and the secret hope that someone sees it in my house and thinks I'm one

of those girls who has enough time/wherewithal to moisturize, so clearly I must have my sh*t together. But the reality is the moisturizer never gets used. Though I do use tinted moisturizers as primer for foundation from time to time. Mostly because the font on the packaging is so small that I don't realize it's a tinted moisturizer until after I put it on originally thinking it was a regular foundation. I know, I'm amazing. Currently I'm using Laura Mercier's tinted moisturizer because I got it as a free gift with the purchase of too many other makeup things at Sephora. It's great!

Foundation: I go for high-coverage foundation. I have skin that's really sensitive to temperature and embarrassment, so I blush and have redness constantly. I don't have any real requirements for foundation other than full coverage (or a coverage that can be built up) and the hope that it sort of matches the rest of my body. From what I understand, I have combination skin: it's not overly oily or overly dry. Like my personality, my skin has a hard time making decisions. Very on-brand. My current favorite foundations are Too Faced Born This Way

"Nothing makes a woman more beautiful than the belief that she is beautiful."
—SOPHIA LOREN

"Nothing makes a woman more beautiful than the belief that frozen yogurt has negative calories." —GRACE HELBIG

oil-free foundation, Tarte's Amazonian Clay full-coverage foundation, and L'Oréal's Infallible Pro-Matte foundation.

Under-Eye Concealer:
I'd never fully understood the deal with concealer other than for covering obvious zits and blemishes. I'd see girls using it on their noses and chins and Cupid's bows (that's a thing on your face!) and thought it seemed unnecessary. Until I discovered the witchcraft that is under-eye concealer! My overly anxious brain and excessive caffeine intake keep me from sleeping as much as a regular human should, but under-eye concealer makes it look like I almost got close to a healthy amount of sleep. I love it. It's the most advanced version of Photoshop I know how to use. I *love* Maybelline's Instant Age Rewind Eraser; it's the one consistent makeup product I've used longer and more often than any other.

Bronzer:
I love bronzer. Bronzer tricks me into thinking I have a healthier lifestyle than I do. When it's used appropriately I feel like it adds such a flattering glow and makes me look like I go outside for *fun*. Ha! But it's tricky, because bronzer can cross a line really easily. You

have to be modest. It's like vanilla extract. The tiniest bit packs a punch. And, for whatever silly reason, when I see someone who's used a flattering amount of bronzer, I assume they have their sh*t together. I don't know why, but the subtle sun-kissed glow gives the illusion that they've just gotten back from a vacation on some cool island I've never heard of before, which was desperately needed because their *wildly* successful amethyst-crystal-crotch-sweatpants line sucks up most of their time and energy throughout the year. What a life. The bronzers I currently love include, but are not limited to (because I constantly buy new brands just to see), Tarte's Amazonian Clay Bronzer in Park Avenue Princess and Benefit's Hoola Matte bronzer.

Blush: I sometimes get hesitant about applying blush, because my face blushes so easily by itself. But I've edited enough videos of myself to know that when I'm not wearing blush or in a state of embarrassment, I look like the Crypt Keeper. So I usually always throw some on. I'm big into Maybelline's Dream Bouncy Blush in Coffee Cake and Tarte's Amazonian Clay 12-Hour Blush in Honeysuckle.

Eyebrow Filler: Only within the last year have I understood the beauty and magic of filling in your eyebrows. I've watched so many makeup tutorials thinking the girls were wasting precious minutes of their lives and mine by filling in their eyebrows,

but now I get it. Eyebrows frame the face. When your eyebrows are filled in, it gives the appearance that your face is more "made up" than it actually is. It's like when you take a dumb Fall Out Boy poster and you put it in a chic, Pinterest-esque frame, suddenly it looks less like a complete piece of juvenile sh*t and more like a purposeful piece of art. My current brow buddies are Urban Decay's Brow Box in Brown Sugar, Tarte's Amazonian Clay Waterproof Brow Mousse in Rich Brown, and Anastasia's Brow Wiz in Medium Brown.

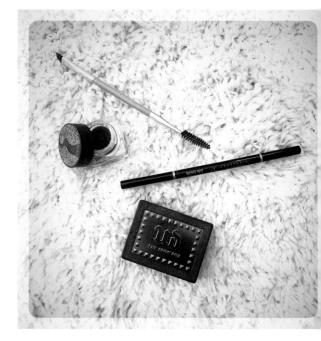

Liquid Eyeliner:

If I don't feel like diving into the eye-shadow game, which can quickly become a disaster for me, I opt for a simple winged look with liquid liner. It's relatively simple, once you get past the initial stage of being awful at applying liquid liner. Don't worry—it's just cat-eye puberty, everyone goes through that phase. I don't experiment with as many liquid liners as I should, but currently I go for Kat Von D's Ink! Liquid Liner in Trooper or L'Oréal's Carbon Black Lineur Intense Brush Tip Liquid Eyeliner.

Mascara:

Mascara is one of my face's BFFs. If I have absolutely no time for makeup, I go for a quick coat of foundation and some mascara. With it, I feel like I look more like a grown human rather than a newborn fetus. It helps compensate for the lack of sleep by making my eyes look wider, suggesting I'm well rested. Basically mascara is that friend that backs up the lies you tell to the rest of the world. Thank you, mascara. Currently I'm in lust with Too Faced Better Than Sex and Tarte's Lights, Camera, Flashes.

Lipstick/Lip Stain:

I rarely put things on my lips unless I'm performing or going to an event, shooting a video, or near French fries. And for the moments I do wear lip things, I opt for a lip stain, on account of the fact that French-fry eating can happen for me at any moment and I might not have time to retouch my lipstick and I'm definitely not passing on the French-fry opportunity. I love Revlon's Just Bitten Balm Stains and really love Too Faced Melted Liquified Long Wear Lipstick in all the colors.

grace expectations

HAIR + MAKEUP

Makeup can say a lot about a person.

It's a great way to express yourself and your style, and an equally great way to accidentally give someone the wrong impression. Your makeup is like a Google Translate between your "essence" and the rest of the world's eager-to-judge-ness.

But I'm here to help. And by now we know that I'm an expert on all things beauty. I wrote a book on it and that's the only qualification necessary to be an expert in my book (literally). So here's what I think your makeup could say about you (individual results may vary).

Lips

Bold Red: I'm confident, I think. Please don't ask me to eat or drink anything that can't be sucked through a straw. I love Taylor Swift, but I also loathe Taylor Swift. She's not that great, you guys. I could do what she does. I took guitar lessons! I mean, one time I hooked up with a guy who looked like Jack White. Still counts. I'm

(trying to be) exciting and mysterious, but if you try any butt stuff, I'll be, like, really sad for days.

Trendy Pink: Yes, I've S'd a bounty of Ds, so what? F*CK YOU. Sike, I wouldn't f*ck you with a ten-foot pole. And yes, I've f*cked a man with a ten-foot pole. JEAL-OUS? Please be my friend. I only eat cranberries. And the moon makes me sad because all it does is continue to circle around the earth and the earth won't even give it the time of day. Literally. I mean SHUT UP. But srsly, will you be my maid of honor when I get married? I don't mean now. OHMYGOD YOU DON'T EVEN LISTEN. I love you! Can I get a double sugar-free Red Bull with triple vodka?

Classic Coral: I could be sixteen, I could be sixty. I'm a wild card. I desperately don't want to be alone. I'm allergic to sauces. Truthfully, I'm just trying to keep up with the Kardashians. I can be sexy, I swear. I'm all about good, clean fun and good, clean fuc-ACCIA BREAD I JUST STUBBED MY TOE. I'm a little clumsy. I forgot I have youth group in the morning. Bye. Don't touch me.

Any Color Outside the Pink/Purple/Red Family: I will ruin you . . . as soon as my Ecstasy wears off and I finish eating the loose pieces of Cinnamon Toast Crunch I found at the bottom of my clear backpack. That, or I fell asleep on my master's thesis while the Wite-Out was still wet. I guess you could say I'm old-school *modest giggle*. Also, by "master's thesis," I mean I have a master and he's writing his thesis. I'm into some weird sex-fetish stuff. But I love cooking.

No Lipstick: I'd rather enhance my brain with thoughts.

or:

I'm running late, so I pinch my lips to make it look like I put stuff on them.

Eyes

Black Winged-Out Liner: I'm mysterious-ish. I don't know how to smize, but when I do this to my eyes, it looks like I do. I love art and bands and whiskey. No, I'll have a margarita, please. I had a fashion blog for a second. I only watch Natalie Portman movies. I'm allergic to potatoes. I'm a vegetarian and you should be, too ... unless we go to Benihana, then I have to get the teriyaki chicken. I tried to make my own soap and it gave me a rash. I buy magazines and take photos of them next to my giant sunglasses to post on Instagram, but I never read them. I don't wear the sunglasses, either. One time I pooped in a trash can. I'm so crazy.

Smokey Eye + Fake Eyelashes: OMG, stop staring. Hello? Look at me! Stop staring! Seriously, look! Now stop it. I had a weird childhood and one too many Cosmos (meaning one), and I'll tell you *all* about it. One time Mom told me if you put your head in the toilet you can hear the ocean and that's why I don't pee in public bathrooms. I'm famous on Instagram. I used a corn dog as a tampon once. I got straight A's in high school, but I don't tell anyone. One time I thought I was at a party at Aaron Carter's house, but it turns out it was a Dave & Buster's. I love hot yoga, hot pants, and hot dogs. But not corn dogs. Did I tell you about the tampon thing?

Bright-Colored Eyeliner: I have an art gallery with an exhibit of dirty socks at the moment. I only eat cheese. Both of my parents are grounded, well-adjusted doctors, but I come from struggle. I love *The Sisterhood of the Traveling Pants*. I didn't wear pants for six months when I was twenty. I don't own a TV. (I own an Apple TV.) I secretly love Nickelback. I'm afraid of singularity, unconscious consumption, and gross birds.

Simple Mascara: I'm super chill. I'm also really difficult. I respect your opinions but I just know they're wrong. I love traveling but I hate crowds and adventure and dirt. My design aesthetic is white. My insides are dark. I'm totally a feminist but that girl over there looks really slutty. I've broken my tailbone six times. When I was eighteen I got a tattoo in Chinese letters that I thought said "free" but apparently it says "fudge." I love yogurt. I sneeze a lot during sex. I took a field trip to the zoo in sixth grade and a peacock sh*t on my Birkenstocks. I'm against zoos but I love laughing.

Glittery Sparkly Disco-Ball-esque: I make a lot of mistakes but it's okay because I know my cryptic religious icon forgives. I've been in twenty-eight beauty pageants and I haven't won any yet because my cryptic religious icon doesn't think it's my time. I eat macaroni and cheese for breakfast. My feet are dyslexic. Oprah, Ryan Seacrest, and Dora the Explorer are inspirations to me. I fell off of a Segway last summer. I've been catfished twice, but the second time didn't really count because it was a dog. I think Nicki Minaj is a role model. I love the WWE. I love supporting charity—I sponsored a toucan in the rain forest last month.

Make
up
your
mind
to discover
how
makeup
enhances
your
natural
beauty.

the bad-hair-day character wheel

HAIR TODAY,
STILL HERE TOMORROW

Bad hair days happen to the best of us.

It's how we know we're humans and not Barbie dolls—a valuable life lesson indeed.

On those days it's immediately clear that we're not going to be the best versions of ourselves; instead we need to choose an alternative. How are we going to salvage this scenario?

This can get really frustrating if you let it. Instead, the best way to handle these types of low-stakes situations is to turn them into a game. Therefore, I've developed the Bad-Hair-Day Character Wheel.

Whether you know it or not, these are all of the character types we automatically assume when we have bad hair days. So rather

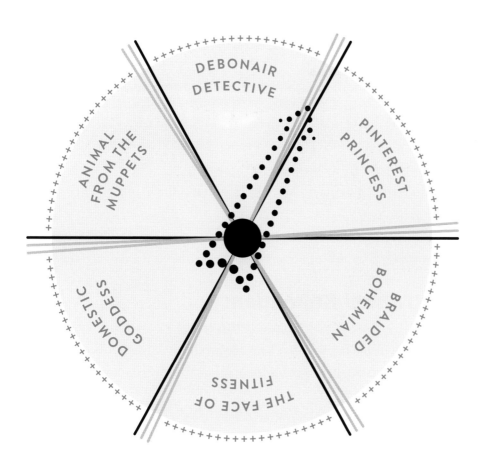

than fight this fate, let's look at it as an opportunity to play out the characters to the best of our abilities. When you wake up and you know your tendrils are against you, spin your Bad-Hair-Day Character Wheel and embrace the outcome.

HERE ARE YOUR POTENTIAL PERSONALITIES

Debonair Detective: Yes, you're wearing a hat. Not because your hair is helpless, but because you're naturally stylish, serious, and mysterious. You're a modern-day Carmen Sandiego. But when someone younger than twenty-six asks you who Carmen

Sandiego is, you tell them you're Vanessa Hudgens. You're dashing and daring and could end up at Coachella at any moment. The fashion police can't touch your crime-solving style. No one knows if you're a real-life Bond Girl or the most stylish person in Witness Protection. But that's how you like it. Hats off to those who figure you out.

HOW-TO: Put on a fedora, felt hat, or other wide-brimmed hat and push all your hair to one side, in either a braid or a loose ponytail.

Braided Bohemian: It looks like fairies broke into your perfectly dimly lit, tulle-netted canopy bed in the middle of the night and braided your hair into an effortlessly beautiful mess. Your flawlessly flawed braid sits atop your unruly but utterly clean locks with a free-spirited presence. Jury's out on whether you're about to wed an unconventional companion in a field of daffodils or about to go to the bank. Braids look way more complicated than they actually are; today you want people to see you like they see your braids. You're cool (but complicated), you're effortless (but affected), and you look like you walked right out of a music festival (but you've never been away from your iPhone long enough to experience anything IRL). It's all about the woven illusion.

HOW-TO: Separate your hair into pigtails and braid; cross braids on top of your head and pin into place; pull out loose strands of hair for an advanced bohemian appearance.

Pinterest Princess: Much like the Braided Bohemian, your style screams, "I woke up like this." Though you don't rely on the classic braid as your base, your tousled tresses suggest you

were too busy making dairy-free dream catchers to bother with a flatiron. Your hairdo looks hippie hapless, not completely hopeless. You have a messy mysteriousness to you that looks accidental, but only you and I need to know that it's a by-product of your bad hair day. The rest of the world can keep on assuming you're either the CEO of Urban Outfitters or some crazy successful social-media-driven street musician.

HOW-TO: Google search chic, boho hairstyles on Pinterest, try to copy.

The Face of Fitness: That messy updo you're sporting leans more toward sports than special occasion. So roll with the punches. Put on some yoga pants and let everyone assume you've been throwing punches all morning rather than your reality of getting knocked out by the spiked punch last night. You're gonna wear a sports bra and a tired expression anyway, why not accessorize it with a Nalgene bottle and create the complete fitness front? Let that sloppy ponytail suggest that you're a Lululemon-outfitted yoga freak, not that you drank too many lemon-drop martinis and spent the night with a Yogi Bear freak.

THE BAD-HAIR-DAY CHARACTER WHEEL

Just make sure you keep your hangover puke down, dawg. (I know that terrible joke probably made you vomit anyway. I'm sorry.)

HOW-TO: Pull hair into a ponytail, spray loose ends with texturizing spray or dry shampoo.

Domestic Goddess: Yes, your hair is a mountain

of mess. But in combination with those perfectly distressed "boyfriend jeans" and some mascara, the masses now think you had a long weekend of HGTV-esque renovations on your spare room while throwing the perfect post-dinner-party-leftovers brunch. No one would dare judge your second-thought strands, assuming it's from the loads of laundry you did while maintaining your manicure. You're *Goop* personified. Yeah, your roots are dirty, but so are the martinis you make. And no one complains about them. You're redefining what it means to be a domestic goddess, but you'd never let that define you.

HOW-TO: Gather hair into a messy bun, pull out random strands around your face, add a bandanna if desired.

Animal from the Muppets: You let it all hang

out. Your sloppy, floppy style paired with your own lack of embarrassment about it is appealing. You create a chaos that is charismatic, a frenzy that's friendly, and a disarray that's so damn desirable. Remember Animal from the Muppets wasn't just a maniac: he was a talented musician. Create a character ruled by her passion rather than her fashion.

HOW-TO: Spray your hair with dry shampoo or texturizing spray; do nothing.

Saturday, Oct. 24, 2015

Dear Diary,

I can't believe it's been a month since we last talked. I'm sorry; time has been flying by here. And there's so much to catch you up on that I don't know where to start.

Previously, in my diary . . .

The last month has been a whirlwind. The building seems to get bigger and more crowded each day, but I've been managing. My class schedule took a second to get used to, but it's okay now. Each day everyone starts in their assigned department stores. I'm in Nordstrom. Which kinda sucks because it's mostly a lot of uptight, skintight formal wear and stilettos in there with me, so I usually just draw in my strings and try to go unnoticed.

The rest of my class schedule isn't too bad. On Mondays, I have history at American Apparel; Tuesdays are English at Barnes & Noble; Wednesdays it's tech ed at Best Buy; Thursdays are health and wellness at GNC; and Fridays I have advanced outdoor discovery at L.L.Bean. Most freshmen sportswear start their athletic studies at Foot Locker, but after reading my entrance essay about the plight of synthetic fabrics afflicted with grass stains, the administration moved me into the advanced class. Which works out awesomely because Birk and Rees are in the class, too! On Saturdays and Sundays, all the freshmen are required to take a class in fashion retail studies, and this semester I'm in Hollister. Which is fine, except I'm the biggest piece of fabric in the whole store and I feel like an ogre. And all the upper-class flannels, who are constantly hungover, just want to turn the lights down and play loud music, so no actual work gets done. Instead, it's usually me, by myself, counting gold armbands in the back of the store while a bunch of halter tops and beanies lie around pretending they *love* whatever annoyingly loud song is playing.

Outside of class, I've been spending most of my free time with Birk and Rees. They've taught me how to snag extra buffalo sauce from the kitchen of Buffalo Wild Wings; shown me where the cleanest public bathrooms are (the kids' section of Barnes & Noble); and even made me a spare key to their secret hideout. They call it their Dream Den—it's the back room of the Hallmark store, where they go to burn incense, listen to CDs of whale sounds, and talk about life while huffing apple-pie candles. The three of us have been meeting in the

Grace's sweatpants
with five different tops!

Dream Den on Wednesdays and Fridays for the past few weeks to talk about our life plan, and we've been meeting in our "BFF" to work out our current big plan.

SHI(R)T! The big plan! OMG, I HAVEN'T TOLD YOU! Sorry, fictional source of guidance, I haven't filled you in on any of it! I'm an idiot. I'm also sweatpants. I've been so *tied* up in my own emotional world that I forgot to fill you in on the bigger updates. I also forgot to work on my puns. Now may I offer you a cart so you can store some of the deep layers of knowledge I'm about to drop on you?

As you know, soon after meeting Rees and Birk, I carelessly dropped the term "Black Friday." But what you don't know is that they quickly encouraged me to never utter those words in the public areas of the MOA again. Yes, the first Friday of the semester they showed me their adolescent "Dream Den," but the second Friday they showed me their more advanced "Brain Fart Fort," an area beneath the Alpaca Connection (yes, an actual store in the MOA), where all the underground stuff goes down. The Alpaca Connection is a store located in between a Nail Trix and a MasterCuts. No one questions anything about the store because no one knows anything about alpacas. Classic Minnesota.

The Brain Fart Fort, or BFF as it is known in the MOA, is a dark market of liberal ideas. It's the place where people can post their open-minded opinions and establish public forums for radical ideas. It's a place to protest freely, to gripe legally, and to complain generously.

What I didn't know was that the BFF is a hotbed of Black Friday activity. Birk and Rees first brought me there after my second L.L.Bean class, in which we learned the value of investing in a puffy vest. After an inTENTs lesson about reinventing your tent, I thought I was heading to the Dream Den with Birk and Rees, but instead they brought me to the Alpaca Connection. I asked, "Why are we here?" And they said, "Because you're the missing piece." I immediately thought we all must have huffed too hard on a hard-cider candle, but they pushed me into a back room and sat me in a dark corner. I started to detect some movement nearby. When my sight settled, I noticed I was in a room with a couple pairs of clogs, a couple pairs of ripped Sears jeggings, and a couple pairs of panty hose. It was a room of misfit outfits. I thought I was being smuggled into a fashion graveyard, but then I remembered that I come from an extremely poor family, so there's no way they could hold me for ransom. After all of my absurd anxiety cleared, I finally whispered, "What do you mean?" and a familiar voice replied. "We're not mean," it said. "We've been waiting for you."

It was the voice of Dr. Scholls.

Ack, someone just threw a red-lined receipt paper roll through my storage door, Diary! That's a very bad sign! Diary, I should just close you right now, but I feel a need to continue to explain the underlying gang warfare, or crew spews, that happen at the MOA. The "threads" versus the "snips" is one of the most infamous rivalries. For years they've butted threads, but they had one day of peace years ago, a day called Black Fri— I gotta go, Diary!

Sincerely,
Sweatpants

Grace's one top with
three different pairs of sweatpants!

choosing glasses

HOW TO FRAME YOUR MEAT MASK

Glasses and sunglasses are lovely accessories that can add layers of style to your look with minimal effort. Growing up, I always thought glasses were *so cool.* So cool, in fact, that in third grade I cheated on my eye test so it seemed like my vision was impaired and I could get them. But I was such a nerd about getting in trouble, or "found out," that instead of just saying a different letter than the ones they showed me in the eye machine, I squinted hard enough so each letter would look like a different letter and I wouldn't actually be lying about what I saw.

I ended up getting glasses but only used them for about a year. My prescription was so minimal that my lenses were practically clear plastic. But it turns out if you don't need glasses, even the tiniest prescription will give you headaches. Which is what started happening to me until I stopped wearing them altogether.

I still think glasses are *so cool.* I have a couple fake pairs that I'm ashamed to admit I wear sometimes when I travel or when I write. Something about them makes me feel smarter, more cultured and more capable . . . of bullsh*tting myself.

Sunglasses, on the other hand, are glasses I'm allowed to wear without shame! And I do. I've collected and lost so many pairs as an

adult that it's become a game to see where they turn up. I could have five pairs one day, zero pairs the next day, and fifteen pairs sitting in the trunk of my car the day after that.

There are plenty of magazine articles and blog posts that teach you which frames are the most flattering on different face shapes. But there aren't a lot of places that tell you which shapes you should avoid. Thank God I'm here.

Round, moon-pie faces: The shape of your face is very reminiscent of a whole uneaten pizza pie. It's a delicious crowd favorite, usually associated with group activities and communal fun. With that, you want to avoid triangular-shaped glasses of any kind. They remind people of individual slices of pizza, which, contrary to the full pie, are usually associated with solo activities and depression. They're also associated with the Illuminati and the food pyramid, which are linked to depression.

Oval, Bert-like faces: The shape of your face is very reminiscent of Bert from *Sesame Street*, or an unbroken egg, both of which have been used as educational resources to warn children about drugs. That said, you want to steer clear of aviators and steam-punk goggles. Aviators remind people of that movie *Avatar*, and it's difficult to watch that movie without feeling like you're on drugs. Steam-punk goggles are associated with raves, which are also hard to endure without feeling like you're on drugs. Also, one of the greatest aviators of all time was Amelia Earhart, and she never looked that great in her steam-punk-esque pilot goggles.

Oblong, heartlike faces: The shape of your face is most similar to an upside-down triangle, reminiscent of a guitar pick or a heart, both of which are associated with love and relationships. Therefore, you want to avoid any phallus- or genitalia-shaped glasses. The combination of your heart-shaped head and phallic frames will cause yourself and others to think about recent relationships, and those thoughts usually spark too many complicated feelings to manage in public—like the lingering bitterness you still have because your ex pointed out that you're a raging narcissist with control issues? Feelings like that.

Square, Lego-head faces: The shape of your face is as wide as it is long. It's most similar to the shape of the apps on your iPhone's home screen, or a piece of bread, which are two things that often challenge a person's self-control. With that in mind, you want to avoid round frames. Round glasses are very reminiscent of Harry Potter, which, when combined with your square head, will remind people that they can't simply cast a spell and eat all the bread they want without consequences, or magically add nonexistent features to their Instagram app. Your round frames will be a sobering reminder that we're all only human.

my jewelry MVPs

I LOVE JEWELRY

Jewelry is an easy way to let the world know

you're trying to make your ensemble more interesting. Or you're trying to cover a stain on your shirt. Or you're trying to use shiny objects to distract from your emotional baggage. Jewelry is fun!

It's also stressful. There's so much jewelry out there and so many ways to wear it, where do you start? When do you add things? When do you take things away? What combinations work best? It's like cooking. And cooking stresses me out. I either add way too many ingredients or absolutely none and decide to order in. To me, people who accessorize well, just like people who cook well, are very impressive. They seem to effortlessly know the best combinations, and when I see their outfit (or taste their food), I'm just like "Well, duh, yeah, that's great. Where did you learn how to do that, witch?" And then I have to apologize for calling them "one of those *real* witches" to their face.

Unfortunately, I don't know the art of accessorizing well enough to give you effective tips or techniques.

Phew, what a refreshingly self-aware book this is!

That was my impersonation of you reading this book. I'm sorry if it seemed offensive. Moving on. (But, like, it was a pretty good impersonation, right?)

What I can show you are the MVPs I reach for on a regular basis. I'm fairly terrible at the jewelry pairing-and-layering thing that a lot of trendy-lady-strangers on Instagram seem so good at. I mean, my idea of pairing a wine with dinner is literally "any wine" with "any food."

Consequently when I add ornaments to my outfit, seventy times out of sixty-nine, I go for one major statement piece (most often a necklace). It gives off the effect of accessorizing in one easy step. It's like bringing a store-bought cheesecake to a dinner party. It's always a crowd favorite, and people put you on the same pedestal as the woman who spent six hours laboring over individual gourmet mac-and-cheese bites. Take that, Krysten with a *y*! I often wear a lot of solid or neutral-color outfits, which lend themselves perfectly to statement necklaces. I also love adding statement necklaces to overly casual (aka sloppy) T-shirts in an attempt to look trendy and like I have nothing to prove. It has that same level of unexpected punch as deep-fried ice cream. It's trashy and tasteful and though you'll never understand the science behind it, you love it.

HERE ARE MY PRINCIPAL PIECES

Statement Necklaces: This lion's head statement necklace from Topshop has been one of my signature go-tos for years. I love that it mixes metals and that it's interesting. It's loud and simple, which is the exact opposite of how I would describe my own personality. I'm so quiet and complicated I annoy myself. This was the first necklace I let myself splurge on at Topshop a few years ago. It was almost $30 and that was an insane amount of money to spend on an item I would most certainly instantly lose or ruin. I am especially poor at managing jewelry, which is why I don't value it the same way a lot of other women might. I can barely keep track of my passport, let alone various tiny pieces of metal. In the past, family members have gifted me nice pieces of jewelry to celebrate things like my college graduation, but my track record with nice things keeps me from ever wearing them. They become anxiety grenades: boxes that I have to try to keep track of because I KNOW the gift giver will ask me at the next family party how they're doing and I'll have to pretend that "They're great, I'm just not wearing them today because I wanted to give them a break."

But this lion necklace was the first pricier piece of jewelry I bought in an attempt to treat my adult self. Necklaces were noticeably the item of jewelry I wore most frequently, so it only made sense to start investing in those. And this particular piece was the start. It's humble and bold and trendy and timeless. I've worn this necklace to book signings, TV tapings, conventions, nights out, and in too many videos. I've worn it so much that the gold is fading to silver and the silver to gold. It's a piece that a broad spectrum of people have complimented, both fashionable and fashion-phobic. I should probably find a replacement since it's showing its age, but

I'm planning to stay loyal until it falls apart completely. So, if you see me wearing this, please pretend it's new.

This winged necklace was bought around the same time as the lion, but from H&M, so it was slightly cheaper. In addition to the lion's head, these two statement necklaces represent my overall jewelry aesthetic as well as the average level of care I take in my accessories. I've worn it just as much as the lion, which you can see from the mixed metal gradient that has developed. When I first noticed that happening, I got bummed and stopped wearing this piece, thinking it had run its course. But because of my forgetfulness, I never actually threw the piece away and have now convinced myself that the decomposition makes the necklace look purposefully aged, like it could be an authentic eighties heirloom. Like the Metallica T-shirts that fifteen-year-olds buy from Forever 21.

In addition, my pineapple necklace is my accessory aesthetic to the core. I was in Toronto for an Internet festival in 2013 and saw it in a Topshop. I fell in love so hard so fast. It's showy and stupid and fashionable and funny. I immediately bought it and wore it with a sweatshirt to a bunch of my events that weekend. I loved it. Not only did I get compliments on it, but also when people hugged me too hard, it hurt. Style and self-defense? Sign me up forever. However, in the signature fashion of my signature items, I broke it immediately. The closure chain fell off in the middle of a meet-and-greet, which was easily rectified because it could be hooked closed to any part of its main chain. But then one of the pineapples broke off. Which was a bummer because the necklace wasn't cheap. But it can still be fixed; I just haven't fixed it in the last two years, for some reason. I guess this is an elaborate note to myself to fix it. So, if you see me wearing this, please commend me on fixing it.

Sentimental Items:
I have very few sentimental items, especially jewelry, on account of my awful track record at keeping small possessions. I also have an ability to "stash and trash" like no other. I don't know many other people like this, so please enlighten me if it is common, but I'm above average at both gathering too many things (stashing) and at throwing everything away at once (trashing). It's a very extremist mentality. I'll keep a bunch of T-shirts from ten years ago thinking there's some sort of nostalgia surrounding them, but as soon as the nostalgia wavers, I'll throw all of them away, along with 90 percent of my entire wardrobe just to get a "fresh start." At my house, spring cleaning happens twice every season. However, these two jewelry items are special because significant people in my life have gifted them to me and I've managed to keep them in decent-ish condition. I'm practically a real adult!

My grandmom left me the pocket-watch necklace after she passed. I remember sitting on her lap when I was really young, maybe seven or eight, and she showed me what time it was in her tiny clock necklace. I was so in awe of it that I simply responded, "Can I have that?" I had never seen a necklace like it before and I wasn't one to selfishly beg, but apparently I could bluntly demand. My grandmom laughed and simply responded, "When I die, Grace, you can have this." And I don't remember ever talking with her about it again. After she died, when I was in my midtwenties, my dad told me she left me something, and sure enough, it was the tiny clock necklace. Turns out my grandmom loved martinis and keeping her word. I love this necklace but I hardly ever wear it; it's become more of a personal conversation piece. I love knowing I have it and I love knowing where I got it. It's my small slice of special.

Same with the gold ring I have with the emerald stone. A significant other gave it to me during an extremely formative time of my life. The difference is, I wear the ring almost every day. It's a lovely reminder of what "caring" means, both from the person who gifted it to me, and myself because I've been able to care for a nice item over a significant amount of time. The ring represents something very sweet and personal and inspirational.

The Cheap Stuff: In addition to statement necklaces and a couple sentimental pieces, inexpensive rings are my go-to accessories. Aside from my emerald ring, my ring collection is composed of cheap, kitschy costume pieces all damn day. I buy a lot of them from

H&M or Forever 21–type places; I go for low-cost, trendy pieces that I'm okay with eventually losing. Because I will. And I wish I could say I constantly lose my possessions because I maintain some spiritual practice about all things being transient, but I lose my possessions because I maintain irresponsibility. I like rings that make a subtle statement; comical pieces that allow a stranger to focus on my quirky sense of style rather than my poor sense of smell. These items are always in rotation because I'm constantly forgetting them in various hotel rooms and random bags, or corroding their weak patinas with various showers and random laundry washings. So, if you see me, remind me to take better care of my rings.

vintage grace

MY BAG, MY BODY, MYSELF

When I was in sixth grade, I made my first foray into the field of bags.

Sixth grade was the highest grade of our elementary school; after that, you moved on to seventh grade at the regional high school, which brought together students from three districts. So as sixth graders, you felt pretty badass. And even more badass because at the end of that year you got to take the annual sixth-grade class trip to Washington, DC.

The class trip to DC was a big deal. It was a *day trip*. Meaning it wasn't our average midweek field trip where we'd shuffle onto a yellow school bus to see some old cannons or cheesy Civil War reenactments. Nuh-uh. For our end-of-the-year DC trip we were taking a GREYHOUND bus with, get this, AIR-CONDITIONING. We'd leave early Saturday morning from the parking lot of our South Jersey school and return late Saturday night. It was the most time we'd spent away from our parents (unless they volunteered to chaperone—gag!) and the most time we'd spent with each other IRL. It all felt very adult. Our pre-hormones were RAGING.

All of us girls had been planning our outfits and accessories for weeks. It was as exciting as prepping for a dance . . . during the daytime . . . outside . . . in the early June heat . . . while pretending to be interested in the Washington Monument. It was my first-ever day trip and the first real trip that I didn't have to bring my backpack for. We didn't need any books or folders, so it wasn't necessary. But surely I needed a bag. Girls need bags. It's simple physics. So I went to the mall to choose the perfect thing. And BOOOOOOY, did I. I walked right into Claire's fashion jewelry and accessories and I bought myself a backpack shaped like a stuffed-animal frog with a zipper just below its neck.

F*CKING. NAILED. IT.

I got home, ran to my room, threw the frog over my shoulders, looked into my dirty, smudgy mirror, and thought I was HOT SH*T (or whatever the midnineties equivalent of "hot sh*t" was). Mind you, this was the peak era of the Spice Girls. Pleather and glitter were gods and anything tacky was trendy. Thus my absolute need to own this bright green furry frog backpack.

The Saturday of the DC adventure came and I woke up and got myself together. I have no memory of what I wore, but it didn't matter because my frog bag was the real hero. Though the actual contents of the frog were pretty pathetic: a disposable camera (and not in a hipster way, again, PRE-INTERNET), some money my mom gave me for meals and souvenirs, a notebook, and some cheap lip gloss. But the frog held all of those essentials without a single struggle. The frog was too good.

We arrived at the school and started piling into the Greyhound bus bright and early. A few friends complimented my frog and those who didn't were thinking about how cool it was in their heads, I could just tell. The bus-loading scene was an energetic frenzy of who was sitting with who and where (we'd been choosing our bus buddy for weeks through notes and various lunchtime/recess debates). We were finally all settled and on the road. Immediately, drunk on parentless excitement, everyone started busting out their disposable cameras, wasting tens of photos. Caught up in the commotion, I whipped open the throat of the frog (a gruesome place for a zipper, in hindsight) and grabbed my camera to take a couple terribly angled shots. And after I returned my throwaway cam to the belly of the beast, I tried to close up the throat. No dice. The zipper was caught in a huge tuft of green frog fur, and no matter how hard I, or my bus buddy, Crystal, pulled, we couldn't get it closed.

FIVE MINUTES INTO THE TRIP AND THE FROG WAS BROKEN.

I wasn't one to call attention to myself, even though the initial purchase of the frog suggests otherwise, so I spent the rest of the day trying to play off awkwardly holding the backpack over one shoulder so my precious belongings wouldn't spill out and others wouldn't see that the zipper was broken. Sadly, I never wore the frog again.

I did (and do), however, continue to experiment with bags. They're one of the most useful accessories a person can own. A handbag is the storage closet of the soul. They're miraculous things, really. They can hold tampons and secrets all at once. They can be private and practical and personal, and fashionable and functional and difficult. I think they're truly a reflection of the human they help. For example, my first bag was a useless, broken plush toy, and currently most of my bags are full of trash and receipts and empty travel-sized bottles of Poo-Pourri. I may as well be carrying around a tiny hand mirror.

grace expectations

THE SIX BAGS OF THE ZODIAC

Which bag are you?

Traditional (Structured) Shoulder Bag

YOU: You're well thought out, you're classic, you're traditional; you're practical with a sense of style. You've always been there for the people who need it most even though oftentimes they don't see how much you do for them. Some say you can be uptight, but others say that in the right situation you can be easy, breezy, hands-free sleazy! You're good at what you do and you're not trying to be something you're not. You can be simple and you can be showy. You can be salt *and* you can be pepper. Hell, you can be paprika when you really want to be. You've got the best of both worlds. And the worst. Your work can be repeatedly effortless or completely irregular. You can be monotonous and mischievous. You're creative and uninspiring. Exciting and ordinary. Fashionable and a faux pas. You're the first choice and a charity case. You're fun and humdrum. What a life of contrasts!

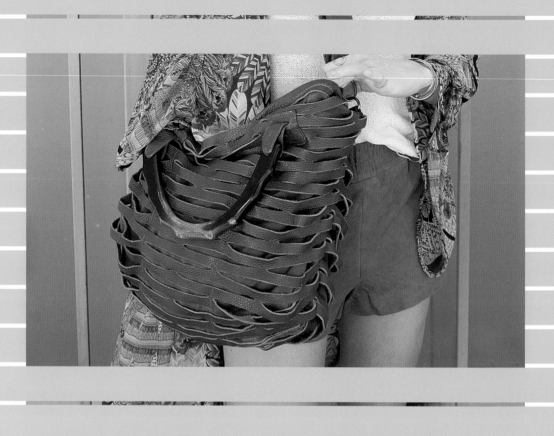

YOUR LOVE LIFE: Your love life is a roller coaster. It's up, it's down... it's gone in the morning (ʜᴇʏᴏ!). You're either tethered to someone for life or a whirling dervish of romantic disaster. You keep it all inside, but you can only hold so much. You're always there for others; it's about time you found your own shoulder to lean on. You're one in a million. Literally. Probably one in millions. Billions, even. Don't let that faze you. Find your match. Find someone who will appreciate you. Someone who will take care of you. Someone who will build you up and show you off. Someone who's proud of you and knows what you're capable of. You may have found that already without even realizing it.

YOUR FUTURE: Expect change in the most consistent way. When Jupiter aligns with Saturn's fourth house on the eighteenth, you'll feel a sense of tied-down freedom in all aspects of your world. Be on the lookout for cats. All kinds. Everywhere. They're the key to your happiness. Also, don't be downtrodden late in the month when Venus shines through Pluto's moon phase and you find out all your friends got tattoos without you. Their tattoos are ugly. And that's not you. You're a classic. And don't forget to reconnect with the family unit—they might hold the key to your love life this summer. Or they don't. Just don't forget about the cats.

Hobo/Slouchy

YOU: You're a free spirit. You're passionate and uninhibited. You're organically spontaneous and naturally fanatical. You're happy-go-lucky and happy-to-go-anywhere, at any time. There's more to you than what people assume and you often impress others with the amount of knowledge you hold. You're a collector. A gatherer. Some say hoarder; you say "prepared-for-anything-er." You're well-meaning but sometimes too assertive. You're tough but you have a soft side. You're flexible but sometimes a little awkward. You're sharp but sometimes uneven. You're messy. Period. You're cluttered. Minimalism is just not in the cards for you. You think about too much too often to have empty space in your life. If cleanliness is next to godliness, it's a good thing you don't identify with any specific religion. You're on a mission of success and self-discovery. And it's a mission you've chosen to accept and you're impassioned to complete it. You're the Tom Cruise of self-actualizing.

YOUR LOVE LIFE: You're not meant to sow your wild oats just yet. You're too busy growing your own oats on your organic, free-range, cage-free, meatless farm. You crop it like it's hot. Monogamous love, to you, is like a music festival. It's a lot of hype. It's hard work to get into, it's kind of boring and uncomfortable when you're in it, and you sleep better when it's over. Eventually you'll settle down, but for now, you're a migration station. You're all about that spring fling. And that summer fling. And that fall and winter fling, too. Most of your romantic interests will get lost in the sauce, but the most interesting ones will add layers of flavor to your life.

YOUR FUTURE: The indigo moon meets with Mars and lets you know that business is booming in the third quarter. Have ideas about a start-up? Well, start it up! And put your friends to work! Friends are like family, but better because you got to choose them. And you've chosen them to lay the foundation of your fiscal success. Brrr, it's going to be a rainy season in the financial department for you this winter. This summer Saturn lays eyes on the fourth house of Pluto; expect a rash. A weird one. This year is all about health and wealth. Remember, your body is a temple. And there's a price for admission.

Backpack

YOU: You're timeless. You're a people pleaser. You're a hard worker. You strive to make others' lives easier. You pride yourself on being rational, reasonable, and prepared. You're loyal to no end. You want the people close to you to know you've got their back. You're not necessarily described as stylish, but your fashion stems from your function. You like to blend in. You've gone through some phases here and there, but you always come back to your center. You're not one for stuffy, formal occasions; you prefer getting down and dirty in some fresh air. You're a family person; and even your friends say you feel more like family to them than most of their own relatives. You're dedicated to your work, and it pays off. Finishing projects is in your blood. Granted, it's not the most glamorous work in the world, but you like it. You're most comfortable when you're working. You're great at focusing. You stay away from dramatic situations. You're able to compartmentalize your feelings. It's a blessing and a curse. You tend to be robotic at times and that can push people away. But sometimes you're happiest when you're alone.

YOUR LOVE LIFE: You like your relationships like you like your rustic abode: full of mahogany . . . I mean monogamy. BOTH. When you're in a relationship, you're in it for the long haul. You're more traditional that way. You like being paired up, you find comfort in having a companion. You're pretty set in your ways, so the best relationships are the ones that challenge you and push you past your comfort zone. Be wary of the ones that try to turn you into something you're not. Rather, celebrate the partners who push you to your potential and appreciate everything you do. You're not afraid of hard work at work, so don't shy away from the effort it takes to maintain a happy, fulfilled partnership. You're best when you're balanced. All work and no play can make you dull, so don't be afraid to "loosen the straps" on occasion, if you get what I mean? . . . You don't, do you? Yeah, you've never been the best at getting a joke. I mean be sexy. Don't be afraid to unpack the goods and let loose!

YOUR FUTURE: Jupiter heads into the sixth floor of Venus, so be prepared for a winter of love. Clean out those closets and call the chimney sweep because it's time to lighten the load and stop kissing toads. Lady Luck flies into your new moon this spring with some helpful news about a loved one's illness—it's cured! But that doesn't mean you care. Don't be afraid to get a pet to heal your anxiety. Stay away from bagels, they always lead you astray. When Venus finally resurfaces on the thirtieth, make sure you're not going to a surprise party, or you'll really be in for a surprise: scabies! And not in the place you expect them. Keep ham in your refrigerator.

Clutch

YOU: You're feisty. You're fashionable. You're forward-thinking. You're a free spirit. You can't be chained down, but you love feeling close and needed by the ones you love. For a brief moment of time. You're a social butterfly. You're able to float from social scene to social scene with ease. You don't hold grudges because you just don't have time for that. You live life in the fast lane. You're always on the go. You pride yourself on being able to handle anything, even though some say you need to get a handle on yourself. You work hard, you play hard, you work out hard, you lay hard. HEYO! You get bored easily, so you have to keep things spicy. Occasionally you push it a little too far and might lose yourself. But it's nothing a detox can't fix. You're attracted to fast, fancy fun. It happens. You're a minimalist. You try to surround yourself with only the essentials; extraneous things (like extraneous people) slow you down. People tend to love you or hate you, but that's never bothered you. Some might tell you to get a grip. But to you, that's jealousy talking. You're clutch.

YOUR LOVE LIFE: Your love life is hot and cold; you can be held too close one second and tossed aside the next. But that's how you thrive. You're used to moving forward and not looking back.

Your ability to transition from one significant other to the next is impressive, but it leaves you less than fulfilled. Maybe it's because you've always operated with next to no empty emotional space for others to occupy. Your internal access is restricted, and if someone is able to break through, there's no room for him or her to stay for long. Which is fine because you've taught yourself to believe that the intense life you live is satisfying enough. You're more attracted to success than sex. The only anal you're into is your own anal-retentiveness.

YOUR FUTURE: Beware the ides of March. When Neptune unleashes its third moon rising into the zenith of Mercury, a career initiative you thought was stable is about to face an earthquake. Find a suitable doorway to stand in now. Tomatoes will present themselves in mysterious ways—pay attention to them. This spring/

summer might be the time to clear your brain of all of those relationship cobwebs and dust off the old cowboy boots. The fall harvest will truly be a harvest indeed. Farmers, farmers, farmers! But don't forget to stop and smell the roses. But don't stop for too long because you're on private property! Look into real estate as a new outlet. You might find love in hopeless hallways. Love it, don't list it!

Novelty Bag

YOU: You cannot NOT express yourself. You eat, sleep, and bleed artistry. If you stop your creativity, you'll die. And not in, like, a performance-art-piece kind of way. How cliché. Your whole life is one big creative process. You think outside the box, you create outside the box, you might have actually lived in a box for a month or two—it was a social experiment! You're so quirky that ukuleles fall apart and suspenders snap if you get too close to them. You invented the mustache. You can be a LOT for people to handle. But you already know this and you don't try to make any apologies for it. You surprise people with your self-awareness. But you have great relationships with the people who *can* handle you. They don't mock your art, they appreciate it. You either come from a huge family or a tiny family. And if your family isn't present, your friends have fulfilled that role in your life. You live for attention, you exist to be seen, you thrive on eyes. You're a great party guest and the epitome of a "plus one." Just by association you make boring people seem interesting, you make unexciting events seem stimulating, you'll probably never read this book because you're too busy turning a full-sized wheelbarrow into a necklace.

YOUR LOVE LIFE: Your love life is as imaginative as your platonic life. Love is another form of expression for you. You love passionately. But you have difficulty maintaining anything long term because, quite frankly, you're a flight risk. Potential partners are weary of your wandering. But your whimsy has never ceased to attract others. Your freedom and eccentricity are electrifying to those still stuck in their own ways. You don't "love 'em and leave 'em" per se, you just "love 'em and playfully move on to the next creatively stimulating thing." You don't limit your capacity for traditional romantic relationships, but your fanciful way can sometimes be a crutch to keep yourself from ever getting hurt. Don't be afraid to make yourself vulnerable. Exposing and challenging that insecurity can be very artistic.

YOUR FUTURE: Well, well, well, if it isn't Venus's fifth dimension exploding all over your full moons this upcoming summer. Expect social circles to become squares, so don't cut corners. It might seem like your life is becoming a reality program, and that's because it is! Cancel your subscription before it starts. Hats are your best friend when an experimental haircut goes awry. Don't forget to back up your hard drive. When Saturn's left ring descends into your third town house, love is going to jump at you like a dog in a burrito store. Apologies go a long way this winter, wear yours loud and proud and plowed!

No Bag

YOU: You didn't buy this book.

YOUR LOVE LIFE: Either very normal or very abnormal, but it doesn't make too much sense for me to try to explain it because you didn't buy this book.

YOUR FUTURE: With Mercury in retrograde, you'll spend your time doing anything other than reading this book.

Saturday, Oct. 31, 2015

Dear Diary,

I have a limited amount of time to spend with you right now. But trust me that this *cinched* time we have isn't a *waist*. See, I'm calm: I'm still making puns. I've been stupid-busy, Diary. The combination of my normal class schedule together with my secret fight against the anticlassist schedule has been a difficult balance. I never thought I'd spend my first few weeks at the MOA leading a "material" militia, but here I am!

Tonight in the BFF (the Brain Fart Fort—I know, I wish the acronym was different, too), a familiar voice came from the shadows saying they'd been waiting for a sign. That voice was Dr. Scholls's.

I didn't understand what was happening. I thought I had eaten some undercooked pork from Benihana and was having a very unimpressive fever dream as a result of food poisoning.

But Dr. Scholls continued to talk with me. He grabbed my drawstrings and started to lead me away, and when I looked back at Birk and Rees, they looked like they were trying to ignore the fact that I'd just audibly farted. And that's when I knew this conversation between Dr. Scholls and me wasn't an accident.

Dr. Scholls told me that G-Wind had made sure that he knew I wasn't dumb, and given that, he should expect me to have suspicions as to why all of this cloak-and-dagger stuff was happening. I said, "Well, obviously it has something to do with Black Friday?" Everyone in the BFF shivered. I looked at them and said, "Oh, you're surprised? Have you really not read my diary!? Get real, misshapen Crocs, I know you have!"

Dr. Scholls continued to try to calm me down. He said that I had a much bigger purpose here than taking classes. He could see that I had the same seemingly passive but completely aggressive attitude as my G-Wind and that that was the fire they needed once again to lead their revolution.

"Again?" I asked.

And then Dr. Scholls went into a very sweet story about G-Wind. It was a story G-Wind had never told me. A story of their passion and their fashion. When they were freshmen at the MOA, they were department-crossed lovers, connected by their determination to assert fabric freedom. G-Wind was in Nordstrom and he was in a Sears department store, but they quickly formed a close bond when they passed each other every Wednesday in the hallway on the way to different body-splash seminars. Eventually, G-Wind threw a note at Dr. Scholls asking him to meet her behind the Alpaca Connection. And that's where their relationship began.

G-Wind would tell Dr. Scholls about her unhappiness with the MOA hierarchy and the newly implemented price-tag systems. She would yelp about department democracy and even tried to take a meeting with the son of her Nordstrom department head, Nordstrom Rack. But it turned out Nordstrom Rack was less than capable. He spit a bunch of randomly discounted tickets and tags at her without rhyme or reason. She went to the student-body presidents, the Brooks Brothers, to talk with them about a retail democracy day. But they wouldn't listen to her. They were too buttoned up.

And that's when she got physical. G-Wind and Dr. Scholls gathered outsiders of all kinds and herded them to the Alpaca Connection. With a good-sized group of unsatisfied garments, she started the Mall Walkers Club. A collection of clothing that gathered on Friday mornings to walk around the grounds as a way to send a message to the more dominant departments. And Dr. Scholls was by her side to make sure her arches were ready for their marches. What a love story!

Eventually the peaceful protests weren't enough. Clothing still had a class structure. Fabrics cost stupid amounts because a *particular person* asked someone to ask someone to ask someone to pay someone to force someone to force someone else to sew a piece of cloth into a certain shape. How dumb! So G-Wind needed to take *real* action. So she concocted Black Friday. A day on which all clothing and accessories were more accessible to the public at reasonable prices. G-Wind and her fashion faction printed sales stickers, discount tags, and clearance signs and put them everywhere: on objects, in store windows, in dressing rooms...you name it, it was discounted! They alerted any media they could, and all the media they couldn't get to was aware of the markdown mayhem within hours. The news spread like wildfire.

And it was all because of my G-Wind.

Dr. Scholls finished recounting the story with a heavy sigh, and it all made sense. He and my G-Wind had had an intense and radically political romance. How beautifully tiring and tragic.

Black Friday was meant to be a brilliant celebration, but instead it became a dark day. The crowds and pandemonium caused by reduced prices resulted in chaos in the fashion food chain. Upper-class apparel freaked out and G-Wind was kicked out of the school.

"I was crushed when she left. It felt like someone ripped out my sole," said Dr. Scholls.

His pun, Diary, not mine!

But Dr. Scholls went on to tell me that he believed G-Wind's legacy lives on. G-Wind had started a movement, and although it seemed to die out after a while, it turns out it's only been waiting for a comeback.

"The anniversary of the first Black Friday is less than a month away. Underground apparel has been hoping for an uprising for years," Dr. Scholls said. "They've just needed someone competent and comfortable enough to take the lead."

"And what's more comfortable than sweatpants?" asked Rees, walking into the room like I WOULDN'T THINK IT WAS THE MOST CONVENIENTLY SEXY THING HE'D EVER DONE.

Rees was followed by what looked like tens but quickly became hundreds of pieces of misfit merchandise, all of them looking at me. Up until this moment, not a single person, other than Birk and Rees, had acknowledged my presence in this academy, but once they find out I'm the granddaughter of G-Wind, I suddenly have the weight of an entire wardrobe on my hips. That's an insane amount of pressure.

But you know what? My hips don't lie.

"Let's print the price tags," I said, and the eccentric ensembles exulted.

And I'm pretty sure Rees gave me a sexy look, but all the single socks kept throwing themselves in the air and I couldn't get a clear look at him, and it was pissing me off. Anyway, gotta go prep for the revolution. TTYL, Diary!

Sincerely,
Sweatpants

my BFFs

BEST FEET FRIENDS

When I like something, I don't just "like" it.

I really like it. I like it to the core, continuously, until I hate it. If you haven't registered by now, I binge. I binge on "sh*itty" pop songs, graphic T-shirts, TV shows, varieties of hummus, you name it. I also binge on shoes. When I get a new pair that I love, I wear them with everything and to everything I possibly can, until I've worn them out completely or have found another pair more interesting. What does that say about my love life? Eeesh. Stop analyzing. I go for basic shoes that can be worn with a decently wide variety of outfits. Of course, "can be worn" is subjective, but so are what I actually consider "outfits."

HERE ARE MY CURRENT BFFS (BEST FEET FRIENDS)

Black Booties: Flat, black, pointed-toe ankle boots from Zara ($30 on sale). These have been real champions for me. They're comfortable, they look like I care more than someone wearing sneakers, and they go with everything. I've worn these friends to meetings, to the movies, and to red-carpet events. They have a pointed toe, which for some reason always makes me think about kicking people in their scrotums, but in the world of fashion the pointed toe looks posh and powerful. They also have zippers on the

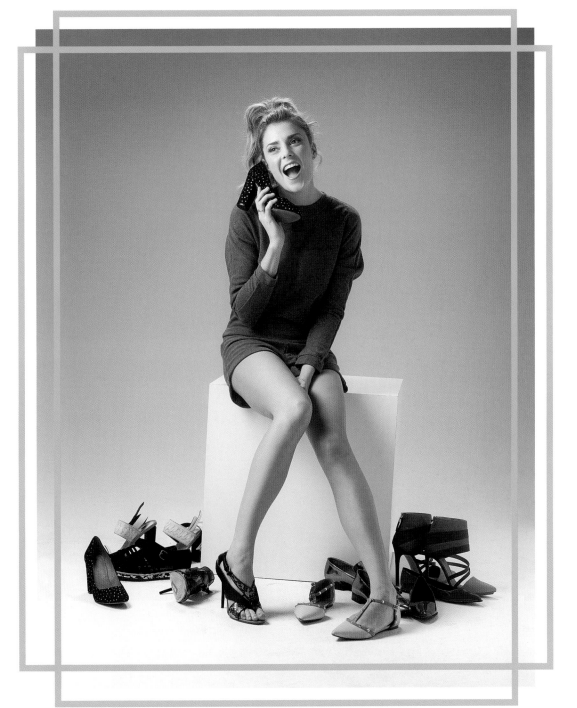

inner heel, which make getting them on and off extremely easy. I've had ankle boots without that feature and they're the worst. Getting them on is like trying to get your dog to talk with you about your concerns for Sonja Morgan's new luxury clothing line on the upcoming season of *The Real Housewives of New York*. It's a struggle. But these are great! They give off that self-aware-wicked-witch-who-knows-you-can't-get-as-much-wickedness-done-in-heels meets Victoria-Beckham-on-a-rest-day vibe. They're also just high enough that you can wear ankle socks with them without worrying about the socks poking out like weirdos. And socks are necessary for a shoe like this. These things are the breeding grounds of beefy feet odors—do not go command-toe here.

White Chucks:
White, low-top Converse Chuck Taylor All-Star sneakers ($50). These seem to be a staple in a lot of closets. They weren't always a staple in mine, not this exact shoe, but I've always had some sort of casual-sneaker option in my top shoe rotation. They're easy. They're cute. They suggest you're more unconcerned and blasé than you actually are. I read in Alexa Chung's book *It* (which I

really enjoyed) that every time she got a new pair of Chucks she'd rub them in the dirt so they didn't look so nerdy and new. And now that's what I do. There's something about a well-worn pair of sneakers without a dank foot stink that makes a person appear traveled and trendy without trying. "Effortlessness" seems to be a thing we strive for; I know I do. But there are fine lines between effortless and straight-up sloppy, and effortless and overworked. A great pair of understated sneakers helps me find middle ground. Also, I really like pairing shoes like this with dresses and skirts and slightly fancier items. It's like sea salt on chocolate. People lose their damn minds because it's unexpected, but somehow it works.

Ballet Flats: Nude, leather ballet flats from Topshop ($25). These are my ride-or-dies. These shoes have seen some sh*t in their day. Well, their elders have. I end up buying a new pair of this exact shoe every six months or so due to wear and tear and stains and stinks. These are my everyday go-tos when zipping or lacing something is just too much stress. What a life! They're comfortable, they're stylish and subtle and made really well for the price.

A lot of shoes call themselves ballet *flats* but they have the smallest of wedges just under the heel—I'm talking centimeters. And I'm not normally a stickler for the details, but that bothers me. It's like someone with one rogue nose hair. You just wanna get it out of there! (Just me? *C'est la vie.*) But these guys, these are ballet FLATS. They live up to their name. They're also extremely universal. You can wear them to a wide spectrum of events with a wide spectrum of clothing. They're like that friend who makes the perfect plus one; they can blend into any environment and get along with anyone. They're always there for you. Even when you abandon them to gallivant around with heels that YOU BOTH KNOW are out of your league. And when you inevitably come back to them, they won't even judge you. God, they're so good. Note to self: get your nude ballet flats an Edible Arrangement—they do a lot for you.

Almost-Could-Be-Heels: Black, studded flats

with ankle straps from Zara ($50). These are what I use to trick people into thinking I'm wearing heels. I bought these on a "whim" in NYC a few months ago when I was getting ready for an event and had one of those moments where I classically thought *I didn't pack any shoes I like!* (aka I wanted any reason to go to the Zara around the corner from the hotel I was staying at). When I walked in, I saw these, thought they might be a little much, got them anyway, and when I wore them to the event, I got a surprising number of compliments.

"You can never take too much care over the choice of your shoes. Too many women think that they are unimportant, but the real proof of an elegant woman is what is on her feet."
—CHRISTIAN DIOR

"The real proof of an elegant woman is her ability not to drunk-tweet."
—GRACE HELBIG

(Any compliment to me is a surprise, for myself and the person giving it—for them it's a surprise since I'm incredibly awful at taking compliments. "I like your shoes, Grace." "HOW DARE YOU!") I've worn them to a few other events, too, and again, received some really nice compliments. So unless it's some extremely mild prank people are playing on me, I like these shoes.

I think people like these shoes because they're more interesting than your average plain flat, but they're still somehow simple. I've worn them with a range of casual and fancy attire. And they're comfortable. Really comfortable. I usually don't like ankle straps because they make my feet feel like they're being strangled by tiny murderers, but these are great. They keep me from having one of those "shoe-pop-off" moments that happen with a lot of flats and sandals that make me feel like an out-of-control idiot. Not these. Another small detail is that they have gold *and* silver studs, so you can mix and match your jewelry and the hardware on your clothing. For whatever reason, I feel tacky if the zipper or other noticeable metal on my clothing doesn't match the noticeable metal on my shoes. Look at me caring about fashion!

Silver Sling-Backs: Silver kitten heel sling-backs from French Connection ($80 on sale). Technically, these are called the French Connection Kourtney Pump. I always find it silly when shoes are named after humans. I like shoes labeled exactly how

they look. I don't want to order the "Henry Appetizer" at an Outback Steakhouse, I want a Bloomin' Onion. Anyway, these are the closest I get to a favorite in the heel department. These buddies have a two-and-a-half-inch heel, which seem even shorter IRL, like a male actor. The silver color is my version of a "pop of color." They're modern and youthful, but the silver still goes with a lot (as long as the metals match!). I used to reserve the term "sling-back" for cocktails, but turns out, it's great for shoes, too. The sling-back strap makes my foot feel more secure in the shoe, like a seat belt on a roller coaster. Because, like a roller coaster, me in heels is a beautiful disaster of unpredictable ups and downs. I've worn these to a couple red-carpet events and they've been great. In my fantasy brain I see myself wearing these with jeans and a button-down for businesslike meetings, but Reality Grace would probably choose the nude flats or Converse sneakers over them at the last minute. Any farts, these are my go-to heels when I get society-standards-peer-pressured into wearing heels for things.

an open letter to heels

Dear Heels,

I had to put this on paper, because every time I try to say it to your face, you hypnotize me with your good looks and delicate ways and somehow convince me you've changed.

But we both know that isn't true. What I'm trying to say, Heels, is that I don't think we're a good fit. I know this is uncomfortable. But so are we.

At times you lift me up, you make me feel strong and confident. All the ladies love you. Even some men. You want to make me a better person. You want to make my outfit look better on my person. You support my butt when the French fries don't. You help me lie about having a sense of style. You've upped my foot-stomping game when it comes to defending myself against potential predators. You never judge me when I make you role-play that I'm a successful lawyer in the final act of a movie power-walking into a courtroom to defend a case that no one thinks I can win. You make my calves seem like real body parts. You stay constant when my other clothes don't. And for all of that, I thank you.

But at the same time . . .

"I can't concentrate in flats!"
—VICTORIA BECKHAM

"I can dominate in flats."
—GRACE HELBIG

You bring me down at unexpected moments. You cause me emotional pain. You cause my ankles physical pain. You give me delusions of grandeur. You pretend to support me but puss out after twenty minutes. You can't handle your booze. You can't handle *my* booze. You're a financial burden. You've bullied my big toenails into running away more than once. You take up too much room when we travel. You constantly try to sabotage the things I like: sports and the beach and grass and boats and bounce castles and jumping on the bed and playing with my dog and water beds and standing and walking and driving and making guacamole.

So, Heels, I don't know where we stand. Sometimes I can't stand you and sometimes I can't stand in you. You have outstanding qualities, but your impulsiveness makes me standoffish. We're at a standstill. I hope you understand. If you want to reach out, I'll be on standby, standing by the nightstand doing some headstands. Standard.

Staying grounded,
Grace

grace

life...style

life...style

The art of buying, flying, and crying in style.........

The art of leaving your house and holding on to your ha

The art of red carpets, red eyes, and reduced prices.........

The art of not looking like ASS IRL.............

The art of planes, parties, and panties.............

The art of being a *cool* hot mess . . . .

The art of *expanding your wardrobe* without social interaction . . .

The art of seeing the world through *affordable, super-cute rose-colored glasses* . . . .

The art of being a *fancy* sheep . . . .

. . . . The art of doing it yourself, *all of it* . . . .

The art of RSVPs and DIYs from my POV . . .

vintage grace

RED-CARPET RIDICULOUSNESS

When I was younger, along with watching runway shows,

I watched all the award shows and all the Joan Rivers red-carpet coverage I could. I read all the pop culture magazines and blogs about the best dressed, the worst dressed, and everything in between. It all looked so glamorous and so desirable, all I wanted to do when I grew up, along with creating a successful and fulfilling career for myself, was to be invited to red-carpet events. The photos! The exaggerated costume clothing! The hobbing and the nobbing! It all seemed so exciting!

And now, as an actual adult (on paper), I've had the opportunity to attend a small handful of red-carpet events and see what they're really like. The screaming! The sweating! The looks from people wondering if you're important and the walking away when they realize you're not! It's not that exciting!

Let me take you through my experience of—get ready—going to and getting out of a red-carpet event.

Leading up to a red-carpet event is a fun mix of anticipation and anxiety. You have to plan what you're wearing, how you're doing your hair and makeup, how you're getting to and from the event, and the time management of it all. Sometimes I get help from my stylist friend in picking out what I'm going to wear and sometimes I get something on my own because I have control issues LOL. Though whenever I pick out something on my own, there's usually a last-minute panic about whether or not it's too see-through, if I have the right type of underwear for it, if I got deodorant smears all over it, do I even have shoes? Etc., etc., etc. My brain is like a static hamster wheel with a bunch of thoughts piled up on it. All of a sudden it goes from zero to sixty in three seconds and all the thoughts fly off in different directions and nothing gets figured out. When my friend styles me, she considers all the things I never do, so I'm way more prepared in her hands.

Getting ready on the day of the event is probably the most fun part of the experience for me. I have a couple good friends who usually do my hair and makeup at my house beforehand, which keeps me in my comfort zone because they know I rarely shower or sleep, so they make sure to bring ALL the dry shampoos and ALL the under-eye creams and they don't judge my excessive caffeine and Internet intake. Occasionally attendance is organized by a third party and they might end up using their own glam squad to make me seem clean. And that's great, too; I just spend more time repressing my feelings and less time checking my Tumblr tags. It usually turns out okay.

When I get ready with friends, it involves a lot of face masks, conversations about whether one of them might have accidentally gone out with a German serial killer the night before, chips and dips, and a vodka shot for the road. I don't consider myself uptight about my hair and makeup. I always assume people who do hair and makeup for a living understand it much better than I do, so I trust whatever they do to my potato face and mop head. Most times I go for some sort of smokey eye and loose curls. A predictable classic.

After the hair and makeup are done, there's a period of time that I call the putz panic. It's the time when I need to be getting dressed because the car to take me to the event is downstairs but I forgot to shave my legs or put on a fake tan or buy panty liners to put in the armpits of my dress to keep my sweat from leaking through in the ninety-nine-degree heat. The putz panic is a Benny Hill routine of me fumbling around my house desperately trying to cover all my beauty bases. Recently during a putz panic before an event in NYC, I tried to paint my nails at the last minute and after I did I realized I hadn't put my bra on. I ended up going to the event braless after smearing reddish-orange nail polish all over my back. But I forgot that my outfit had a cutout in the back and at the event's after-party my friend said she noticed my orange bra when I was onstage and she loved that I matched it to my orange shoes. I told her it wasn't a bra, it was nail polish, and we both agreed that that accident could have been a hell of a lot worse.

After the putz panic, after I've frantically grabbed any clutch-like purse I can find, after I've smeared whatever tanning liquids are in sight on my person, after I've been sprayed and buffed and teased and sprayed again and varnished and sandblasted and sprayed a final time, I dump some alcohol into my mouth and make a run for the car. It's more like an awkward, flustered stumble to the car. I apologize to the driver for being a frazzled fraggle and we're off. It's at that point that I have half a second to figure out what event I'm actually going to, if I'll know anyone there, and what the exit strategy will be. I hate hate hate hate not knowing how to leave a

function. I hate feeling "stuck" when I'm mentally and physically ready to exit a scenario. Control issues LOL. In the car I check social media to see who's at or on their way to the event, whether or not I'm wildly underdressed, and to see if there are any signs of food. Food is hard to come by at red-carpet functions. If you can find it and eat it, you're a champion. I do all this research while trying to lie as flat and stiff as a board so I don't get crotch wrinkles in the waist of my outfit before possibly getting pictures taken. The last thing I need is someone thinking I *sat down* in the car before I got there. How tacky!

The arrival at an event typically goes two ways: smooth and easy or complicated and kind of embarrassing. There are normally a butt-load of black cars and SUVs all vying for an opening to drop off their human cargo at the top of the carpet. Then there are the volunteers and employees of the event wearing lanyards or headphones or both. They're usually very stressed out but try to conceal their stress under aggressive professionalism. They're there to greet the guests and guide them through the red-carpet experience. There's a lot of chaos that happens between them and the agents, managers, and publicists to make sure guests get the appropriate treatment. It's hilarious. There's a lot of yelling and pushing and grabbing and whispering and smiling and air-kissing and overly excited hugging and laughing when people run into people they know. And everyone somehow knows everyone at these things. Or they pretend they do. It's a big Charlotte's Web of social climbing. Plus there are usually fans or people who have gathered to see the guests arriving and walking down the carpet. So there are basically three layers of people-watching at all times. *Everything* is being seen by someone, and it's usually someone with a camera. I never understood how so many female celebrities could get their cootchies caught by a camera while getting out of a car until I finally experienced a red-carpet event firsthand. As soon as you're out of your car, you're sucked into a clusterf*ck that you have no control over. IT'S THE PERFECT ENVIRONMENT FOR ME.

The top of the carpet is the peak of insanity. At least in my experience. Jennifer Lawrence, I'M SURE, has a completely different experience at red-carpet events than I do, so she might not agree with any of this. Which would seriously bum me out because I wouldn't want her to feel like she can't relate to me, making our future friendship even more difficult to realize than it already is.

The beginning of the carpet is where all of the photographers live. And by live I mean scream at strangers. They stand on bleachers, stacked on each other. It's mostly guys who look like a bunch of dads at a barbecue, with the exception of some ladies sprinkled throughout. Without the cameras, they look like they could be a Wells Fargo co-ed softball league. But here they wield a variety of giant lenses with bright flashbulbs and little to no patience with each other or anyone else around them. But hey, that's their job. And because everyone wants their time in the spotlight (literally), there's usually a clog in the pipes at this point. The guests and their wranglers are all shuffling and struggling to get themselves in front of the cameras. If you're paired with a talent escort, most times they have either a sign with your name on it to show the photographers before you step out or they shout your name so they can: (1) correctly label their photos, and (2) decide if they even want to take your picture. Yes. That's a thing. That second reason is a hilariously awkward lesson I've learned about these events. The photographers are there to take pictures of the bigwigs—everyone is just a bunch of Michelle Williamses to them until the Jennifer Lawrences and

Beyoncés show up. So they can *choose* whether or not they want to waste their camera memory on a photo of your face. It's funny and mortifying.

Though I've noticed that if you have an escort showing them your name before you enter the carpet, they lean toward wanting to take your photo since you're obviously important enough for someone to print your name out on a piece of paper.

Here's how it goes down (again, this is only in my experience). You step out onto the carpet and pose (it's like real-life YouTube; you literally post yourself in front of this audience) and the gaggle of dads either pick up their cameras to shoot you, or they pretend to check their cell phones until you leave. WHICH IS extremely Humiliating. It's like that date auction episode on *Saved by the Bell* when that generic background geek (not Screech) goes up on the auction block first and no one bids until Mr. Belding finally throws in fifteen cents to keep things moving. On the red carpet you're the generic background geek on the auction block and eventually the photographers *might* throw you fifteen cents, or a couple snaps, to keep things moving.

It's all so comically degrading. Red carpets and I are like peanut butter and sauerkraut. I'm just not the kind of person to beg for anyone's attention in that way. The idea of asking people to take my picture makes me very uncomfortable. I'm not saying it doesn't work for other people, because it definitely does; it's just not my strong suit. And yes, I know that seems hypocritical with thousands of videos of my own face currently circulating on the Internet. But at least in that scenario there's a transaction: I'm offering you a piece of content that I've created and believe to have entertainment value in exchange for your attention. I can get behind plugging

and promoting in those terms. Now. It took me years to get over the narcissism I associated with self-promotion before I genuinely encouraged people to watch any of my content. But walking the red carpet "promoting" my face, which other people fixed up, in an outfit that other people put on me, still feels strange.

If the photographers decide you're worthy of their camera memory and want to take your photo, they go nuts! They all scream and shout over each other for you to look at their camera. "Grace, over here!" "Grace, c'mon, love, let's get a look up here." "Grace, give me one more to your right. YOUR OTHER RIGHT!" They yell louder and more aggressively until you look their way, and even when they've gotten the photo, they keep yelling. Some tell you how to stand or pose or even give you directions like "jump" or "look over your shoulder" or "no teeth." And because it's such a hectic free-for-all of flashes, *you do it*! At least I have.

I was a guest on *The Tonight Show Starring Jimmy Fallon* a while ago, and when

> "One is never over- or underdressed with a little black dress."
> —KARL LAGERFELD

> "One is never over- or underdressed if they allow their crippling social anxiety to keep them from going to the party altogether."
> —GRACE HELBIG

the interview was done and he threw to commercial break, I gave an awkward thumbs-up to the audience and he put his hand over my thumb and was like "Noooo, don't do that!" And I didn't understand what was happening. To me, I was just doing one of my standard awkward poses, but to him it triggered a flashback. He told me he was on a red carpet for the premiere of a friend's movie once and a photographer told him to give a thumbs-up, but he didn't want to. He thought the gesture was kind of cheesy. But the guy kept asking him over and over to do it, so finally, frustrated, he did it. And he said the next day *that* photo ended up on the cover of some newspaper with a caption about how "Jimmy Fallon sarcastically gives a thumbs-up on the red carpet of [yadda yadda]," basically insinuating that Jimmy wasn't having a good time and didn't want to be there. He had to explain to his friend that the photographer made him do it, and since then he's been on guard about what photographers ask him to do on red carpets. In hindsight, it was very nice of him to try to protect me from my own potential thumbs-up disaster. If only he could follow me everywhere and prevent all of my constant disasters.

Once you get past the main concentration of photogs, you continue to shuffle down the carpet, kind of posing for pictures if other photographers want to take them and sort of meandering around if interviewers want to talk to you. The high-profile celebs usually have a planned-out list of the media outlets they chat with before they get ushered inside. The lower-profile guests wander around and take what comes their way. This is the time when a lot of people socialize and say hello to people they know, or introduce themselves to people they don't. The carpet is a social highway and everyone tries to keep it moving. So you work your way down until you reach the end and are able to head in to the event. Of course, you have the option to bypass the carpet completely and skip out on the hypothetical humiliation altogether. And I've done that before and it's great. But now that I've had more opportunities to assess the ridiculousness of red carpets, I approach them more like a dumb game than a moment that's going change the outcome of my life.

Once you're inside, you're able to assess the food and alcohol situation. It'll usually be obvious pretty quickly whether it's a food-friendly event or not. And if it isn't, that's when I start organizing my exit strategy. I ask myself things like, *Where's the ideal pickup spot? Who's going with me? When's the optimal time to leave? Who should I make sure I say hello to before I go? Who should I Irish goodbye? And ohhhhhh what do I want to eat when I'm out?* That last one's my favorite question.

When I finally exit an event, I figure out my food situation and then I check up on social media to examine any damage from the red-carpet ridiculousness. When I'm home I put on sweatpants, stuff my face, and try to figure out how many videos I can possibly shoot with my hair and makeup still done before my fake eyelashes fall off.

Be at peace
with the fact
that you're not
always going to
look your best,

but if you're
doing
your best,

that look
will always
show through.

BETTER-LOOKING T-SHIRTS

As of late, one of my favorite things to do

is "it" myself: I am a new, dedicated disciple of the church of DIY. One of my go-to hobbies is upgrading plain T-shirts. There are a million YouTube tutorials and Pinterest articles that will show you every possible way you can renovate a second-rate shirt. And now here's my version.

I usually like the way guys' T-shirts fit me better than girls', but I also usually like the designs on lady tees more than dude tees. So what's a consumer like me to do? Here are a couple easy ways you can turn your plain T-shirt into an insane T-shirt (in the constructive, healthy way). I've listed these ideas as both DIY techniques and general life advice, because every lady knows DIY is simply a less recognizable form of self-help. Who needs therapy when you have creativity?

1. **Make sure you're getting enough iron in your diet:** Iron-on letters, decals, and transfer paper are a total game changer. If you look at a lot of the popular shirts on any Nasty Gal, Brandy Melville, or H&M website, chances are you can re-create it. It's so easy to click on a site and buy a trendy T-shirt with invisible credit-card money, but TRUST ME, it's even more rewarding to make your own similar shirt for a fraction of the price and celebrate your savings alone in your house with your dog! Most iron-on letters and transfer paper cost less than $10. You can spell out any *hilariously* clever phrase you want with iron-on letters, or you can print out any *hilariously* clever photo or design you want on transfer paper and iron it onto your shirt. It's so simple a baby could do it (if that baby had very strong wrists and an adultlike caution about hot irons). Also, a lot of craft stores sell iron-on decals that have the potential to be cute! Most recently I ironed a hamburger decal onto a T-shirt and it, indeed, became cute.

✦ Iron a middle finger coming out of a pocket tee.

✦ Spell out "But first, coffee."

✦ Iron the whole sheet of iron-on letters directly onto your T-shirt.

My friend Mamrie did this during a convention and I thought her shirt looked SO COOL. (Yes, I was wearing a jumpsuit that made me look like a sexy auto mechanic at the time, so my taste levels may have been skewed.)

2. We're all going to *dye* some day: Tie-dye! It seems that tie-dyeing is not a dying art. In fact it's a super-cheap, sort of easy way to change up a simple T-shirt. You can buy tie-dyeing kits from craft stores for as cheap as $5. That's cheaper than most pad thai. Just make sure you give yourself ample drying and washing time. Tie-dyeing, like other aspects of the boho-chic look, takes way more time than people might lead you to believe. Those effortless, flower-child waves? Thirty to forty-five minutes at least. That easy, healthy homemade granola? An hour. That casual tie-dyed crop top?

Twenty-four hours of full rinsing and drying.

✦ Having a go-to tie-dyed shirt in your closet comes in handy for *any* college party, Halloween party, music festival, or anywhere there are more than five twenty-year-olds gathered.

3. Leave your mark: Fabric markers are a thing! If you want more freedom with your design, invest in fabric markers. Depending on your design, they'll last you through tens of T-shirts and they wash really well.

✦ Try fake-signed celebrity autographs; if the shirt doesn't turn out well, you can try to sell it on eBay.

✦ Trace a hand onto your shirt, and when someone asks about it, tell them it's "freehand." Tumblr will eat that sh*t up.

✦ In a bind you can always draw permanent penises onto a friend's or enemy's favorite tee.

4. Cut out the excess: Like a house with a poor floor plan, T-shirts can be made into better versions of themselves by removing the unnecessary parts.

Trim the neckline, chop off the sleeves, or fringe the bottom to give a plain shirt new life. It's like when ladies give themselves bangs in order to feel alive. Give your top some literal and metaphorical fringe!

✦ Make your own crop tops. Why pay more for less fabric when you can make your own at home?

5. Make changes that _stick_:

One plain T-shirt plus interesting textiles, trims, and studs plus fabric glue equals the birth of a whole new piece of clothing. Gluing cute trims or faux-fabric pockets or some sensible studs onto simple shirts can make them feel way more expensive. But try to keep the rhinestones and studs to a minimum; the only tacky part of this project should be the glue.

✦ Glue metal studs into the word "lonely" and see what happens!

✦ Make your own homemade Peter Pan collars from pieces of fabric or lace and glue them onto plain T-shirts. It'll have the same whimsical effect without the stunted-adult psychological overtones!

Friday, Nov. 27, 2015

Dear Diary,

It was the night before Black Friday, otherwise known as Thanksgiving to most of the Western world, but to us, it was the eve of our clearance revolution. The second time around. That sounds terrible... Let me try it again. It was a night of gravy-slathered drumsticks to most of the world, but for us, our drums were warming up to welcome the resurrection of the renowned reduction revolt. Ack, one more time. Most of the world was ending their night with warm pie, but we were just warming up for the preamble to our pricing uprising. The reckoning. Okay, whatever, we haven't figured out the best *Bourne Identity*–esque tagline for it, but you get it. It's the night before Black Friday, and to put it lightly, Diary, I AM FREAKING THE F OUT. I've become the Harry Potter of unwanted apparel and the Katniss of clothing misfits. But the thing they don't talk about enough in those novels is how the stress of being an inspirational icon takes a toll on the body. I've been stress-eating Auntie Anne's pretzels and Cinnabons all goddamn day every goddamn day. I hate to say this, Diary, but I'm literally bursting at my seams.

I've been at the BFF all night, sorting sales stickers, organizing media outlets, and going over the finer details of our placement plan. It's exhausting, but truly a beautiful thing to see the power of freethinking fashions weaving together a massive scheme meant to unite fabrics and redesign the outdated order. If we fail in our plan, we've at least succeeded in proving products can come together for a greater good. Or something like that. I don't know, Diary, I'm up to my drawstring in department democracy right now. I needed a break, so I stepped away from the BFF for a second just to loosen my waistband and empty my pockets. And to fill you in. Duh.

So here's how everything's been operating. Last I left you, I became the "sweats of the insurgency." Or "SOTI," as everyone who's affiliated with the MWOA has been calling me. The MWOA is the Mall Walkers of America, the legion my G-Wind started. We communicate with each other in public like we're giving air-kisses: "MWOA, MWOA." We're the expendables of the school, so the faculty and "expensives" (higher-priced, popular products) think it's our way of being sarcastic. Sorta true. But we've been able to communicate under the radar by approaching each other with the signature air-kiss. That signifies that the conversation is in code or should be taken to a more private location.

Over the last month we've upped the organization of the MWOA in prep for the big day. But before I was even brought into the picture, the MWOA had been planning an uprising. They'd been planning one for the last few years, in fact. They just hadn't had the right momentum to make it happen.

I found this out because a couple days ago Rees invited me to get froyo after my History of American Apparel class. As if I didn't have enough stress in my life, now a froyo date?! Yes, "date" is a word I added to this equation. However, it happened on a "day" in time, and if you check any thesaurus, a synonym for "day" is "date," so if you could kindly shove a sock in your mouth and continue listening, that'd be lovely. That day I steamed and lint-rolled myself until I could barely feel my own fabric; I coated myself with Downy Wrinkle Releaser like I needed a herd of dogs to find me in a ditch, and I tied my drawstring so tight I was sucking in more than a factory-refurbished Roomba.

Anyways, we meet for our froyo. And let it be known I was trying SO HARD to eat my stupid *small* froyo with stupid *bananas* in small, slow bites rather than stress-shove the entire thing into my mouth that it's a miracle I was able to pay attention to the actual conversation. I deserve an award. Sorry, I'm getting froyo-unfocused.

During our froyo outing, Rees told me that he had thought Black Friday was going to happen his freshman year. He had heard about the MWOA before he even got to the MOA from an overly distressed, faded cousin. He was raised in a family of overpriced, underdeserving denim. "They don't realize how lucky they are. And THEY'RE *LUCKY JEANS*," he kept saying. He was all about outfit equality, so he made it a point to seek out the MWOA his first day. Luckily (I know, I'm sorry, Diary), he ended up in a Sole-Searching Seminar led by Dr. Scholls that year, and before he knew it, he was introduced to his brand-new BFF.

Rees said Dr. Scholls was totally revved up about the revolution and things seemed to be falling into place, but that October, Dr. S found out he had to be re-heeled. The doctor told the students it was a standard procedure, and they all believed him because he's . . . well, a doctor. But apparently the re-heeling surgery was way more intense than any of them expected and it took him a year and a half to…well, heal. Rees said he wasn't the same person after the surgery. "It was like his balls were gone," Rees said, NOT EVEN REALIZING THE ADORABLE PUN HE MADE, DIARY. GAH! Anyways, because the doctor was on foot-rest, the revolt was on hold, and Rees started to believe the revolution would never happen in his years at the MOA.

But suddenly there was a shift. Rees said he received a letter from Dr. Scholls while he was studying abroad in India (because REES IS PERFECT, IF YOU FORGOT) that simply said, "This year we won't sweat the small stuff, we'll sweat the mall stuff." He couldn't figure out what the letter meant and resigned himself to the idea that Dr. Scholls had officially lost his footing in reality. Until the first day back at the MOA, he had never seen Dr. Scholls as excited about anything as he was greeting me in the parking lot. (Sidenote: Diary, it took everything in my being not to say "I KNOW THE FEEL-ING.") Rees said he started to piece things together, but it wasn't until I stupidly said "Black Friday" out loud that he understood Dr. Scholls's letter loud and clear.

"You're his missing piece, SOTI," Rees started. "You're the reminder that great things come in all packages and that we shouldn't sweat the small stuff…"

Rees was working himself up and started to get out of his chair, but quickly sat back down and regained his cool once he remembered we were in

Grace's sweatpants from H&M

public. He raised his spoon of pumpkin-spice yogurt with toasted almonds and coconut, and said, "We should sweat the mall stuff."

We cheers'd our froyo and I had to keep myself from giving him a standing ovation.

"I feel like I just watched a scene from *Braveheart*," I said.

"Is that the documentary about heart transplants?"

Classic us!

But sweating the mall stuff was exactly what we were going to do. Our group was divided into walkers, stalkers, and talkers. The first group, or walkers, is set up to walk around the mall in the wee hours of the morning distributing the various sales paraphernalia in the various departments of various stores. They were our brawn. The second group, the stalkers, would be stationed at different areas of the mall to stalk the signage and make sure it stayed in place. If someone happened to take it down, they'd put it right back up. If a print went missing, they had replacements on hand stowed in key areas of the mall itself. The last group, the talkers, will spread the word to the public that Black Friday is, in fact, happening. We have talkers contacting major media outlets, posting on blogs, driving through suburbs with signs…There is a rumor that a pizza onesie had access to celebrity vlogger Tyler Oakley and was getting him to mention it in a video. By noon tomorrow, everyone(ish) will know about Black Friday.

And though all of this is so exciting, Diary, I can't help but feel like something's missing. We have walkers, stalkers, and talkers, but we don't have our "shocker." That unique piece that will really ignite the masses.

SQUEAL! You can't see this, Diary, but just as I was typing that last sentence, the door to my storage locker burst open and a shadowy figure just said, "Let's party." The shadowy figure is my G-Wind! She's back! She's the "shocker" we've been missing! I should say hello to her rather than continue to write out exactly what's happening at this present moment! *VIVE LA RÉVOLUTION* or something!

Sincerely,
SOTI

DO I REALLY NEED THIS? FLOWCHART

HOW TO TALK
TO SALESPEOPLE

APPROPRIATE THINGS
TO SAY TO SALESPEOPLE:

1. "No thank you, I'm just browsing."

2. "Sure, I'd love to get a fitting room started."

3. "I'm okay right now, but if I need help I'll make sure to ask you."

4. "Can you point me in the direction of the pants?"

5. "Sure, I'll take a bag. Thanks."

6. "No thanks, I don't need a bag."

7. "Do you validate parking?"

8. "Can I hold these up at the register?"

9. "Are there any additional sales?"

10. "You should subscribe to youtube.com/gracehelbig."

INAPPROPRIATE THINGS
TO SAY TO SALESPEOPLE:

1. "Please eat a thousand dicks."

2. "THIS IS HARASSMENT."

3. "If you give me that bag, you're enabling a very serious problem. I hope you're prepared to handle the consequences of your actions." [SMOKE BOMB]

4. "How many times a day do people tell you that you look like Gary Busey?"

5. "I need to borrow $30 to buy these pants."

6. "NO, I DON'T WANT TO START A DRESSING ROOM. AND I DIDN'T WANT TO BREAK UP WITH STEVE, EITHER, BUT HERE WE ARE."

7. "Carry me."

8. "The total is $97, you say? I have twenty bucks and an unwrapped, unused tampon. Huh?"

9. "Does my extremely obvious hatred of your hovering make my butt look big?"

10. "You should subscribe to youtube.com/harto."

the ten commandments

OF ONLINE SHOPPING

One of my favorite sports is online shopping.

It requires a sharp eye, a supple wrist, some psychological stamina, and a complete aversion to any kind of interaction with humans. It's my version of video games. And with my years and years of training, I've developed a set of guidelines to maximize performance. Here are my Ten Commandments of Online Shopping.

1. **Thou shalt worship many tabs:** My online shopping is never planned. It mostly happens when I see something in a video, in an article, in a pop-up ad, or anything else I'm looking at on the Internet that sparks the shopping fire in me. From there it's CTRL+T, CTRL+T, CTRL+T, CTRL+T. I open a collection of tabs, combing through a flurry of sites, falling deeper and deeper into their rabbit holes of new arrivals, sale codes, and daily deals. The good thing about freely opening as many tabs as my stream-of-shopping-consciousness

wants is that I usually end up psychologically sabotaging myself. I give myself too many choices, which causes me to follow through on zero of them. The act of putting an item in a cart becomes cathartic enough for me to fill whatever void caused the shopping tab spree in the first place. Some might call it cart-thartic. Ha ha! There's no return policy on that joke!

2. **Thou shalt look through reviews and images:** Just like profile pictures on dating websites, clothing in online stores might look extremely different in real life. If there are customer reviews or real customer photos available to look through, DO IT. Recently, I've used the website Rent the Runway, which allows you to rent high-end designer clothing for much cheaper than actually buying it. That website is fan-f*cking-tastic because it encourages the users to review their rentals honestly and accurately and upload real-life images of themselves in the clothing so that you can see all the wins and sins without distraction. It takes so much of the risk out of committing to an item. Imagine if a potential Tinder match had an honest photo of himself next to his gun collection with the caption "Yes, I'm a successful doctor with an adorable French bulldog named Cheeto, but I love guns." It helps you make a clear decision.

3. **Thou shalt not take their convenience in vain:** We shop online because it's convenient. Because it's comfortable and user-friendly. We can take our time, there aren't any store employees asking us if we need help, offering us dressing rooms, or silently judging our choices with their eyes from the other side of the store. Therefore, don't take your personal convenience in vain. Before you check out, if you aren't completely sold on everything in your cart, walk away.

Not physically, ew! Close the tab, take an hour or a day or a week, and then come back to it and see if you still like and need/want what you've picked out. I'll often go to H&M's website and see ten items left in my cart from the last time I was hungover or emotionally weak and wanted the pseudo-satisfaction of investing in business clothes. At the time it felt like I was INVESTING IN MYSELF. But I wasn't. And I can see that now that I've stepped away. Remember there's no pressure to purchase, even though those seizure-inducing pop-ups try to tell you otherwise. Also beware of sites with the one-click purchase feature, like Amazon. They store your credit-card information so you can check out by clicking one button rather than reentering your info. I have "a friend" who's accidentally purchased items by clicking "check out" rather than "back" on several occasions. She's a real dum-dum, I know.

4. **Thou shalt keep holy the holidays:** Holidays are to online shopping what cheat codes are to frustrated gamers. They reduce the struggle. And the struggle is real. Holidays are some of the best times to shop online because discount codes fly like desperate tears on *The Bachelor*. If you're in the market for clothing or home goods or, let's be honest, *anything*, and you're about to dive into some dot-com retail therapy, take a second to check your calendar to see if there's a major (or minor) holiday around the corner. It could make a 40 percent difference for your wallet. Sites love giving discounts for just about anything these days (it gives them a reason to post those obnoxious banner ads on other sites). So don't overlook the minor holidays, or the holidays that might not pertain to you, for sales and coupon codes on things you need (aka want). Maury Povich doesn't have to give you a paternity test for you to get a cocktail shaker for 70 percent off on Father's Day.

The system
works you
all day,
    so work
    the system
    by using
    their coupons.

5. **Honor thy debit- and credit-card limits:** Buying things online can feel like a transactional game with made-up money. You don't hand physical currency to a physical employee, so it can't possibly be real. Which makes it so much easier to click without consequence. This is when the phrase "buyer beware" becomes too real. Keep those tabs open, but make sure you're keeping tabs on how much you're actually spending. With great bargains comes great financial responsibility.

6. **Thou shalt not murder:** Don't murder anyone.

7. **Thou shalt be wary of hangover recovery:** I do some of my greatest Internet-shopping damage when I'm wildly hungover. A hangover is a shame cloud of regret. Thus, when I'm in that state, all I want to do is better myself. And what does that better than *things*! Hangovers usually encourage me to buy juice cleanses I'll only drink half of, workout clothes I'll wear the next time I'm hungover, "goal" clothes I'll never have the courage to wear and won't bother to figure out how to return, inspiring books I'll decorate nightstands with but won't read, bath bombs and facial scrubs I'll pile in cabinets, and lipsticks I'll stare at while wondering what it's like to be a girl who genuinely loves to wear lipstick. When you're in a vulnerable state like a hangover, or even a breakup for that matter, try to be as objective as possible about the objects you want in your life.

8. **Thou shalt find steals:** Holidays aren't the only time when websites offer discount codes. You know how a website asks you to open an account before you check out and then magically you start getting a daily email from them in your junk folder? Well, some of those emails aren't junk. I'm not saying you should inspect every email that comes in, because, yes, a lot of them are, in fact, junk. But some of them have daily deals and discounts just for registering. A couple years ago I made a purchase at gap.com and I registered an account. I always try to check out as a guest because I don't want the spam emails and I don't want to give out my personal info, but this time I registered. After that, I noticed that every time I went to the website, they were offering me a different percentage off my entire order. One day it'd be 25 percent, the next would be 35 percent, and the next would be 15 percent. They make it feel like a game, and for a human who's susceptible to scratch-off lottery tickets, it's a wonderful and terrible game.

✦ Quick tip: If you do a lot of online shopping, I'd suggest making a separate email account to filter those endless promotional emails. It also helps create a catalog of your purchase confirmations so you can access them in one place. It also creates a separation between your "professional" life and your "obsessional" life.

✦ You can also try to Google discount codes for different stores. My mom told me about this a couple years ago and I was shocked that she knew how to Google anything, let alone discount codes. But she's successfully used codes she's found online and the government hasn't knocked down her door yet accusing her of involvement in some illegal digital scandal, so it seems legit in my book.

9. **Thou shalt bear witness to thy return policy:** It's inevitable that some items you purchase online will not live up to the expectations you had for them. Time to return to sender. I'm AWFUL when it comes to returning anything I purchase from the Internet. Instead, I'll rationalize why it's better (easier) to keep it than to take it back. It's six sizes too small? I should keep it because my dog can wear it for Halloween. I literally have three pairs of the same platform sneakers sitting in my closet because I accidentally bought three instead of one on topshop.com and I've been too lazy to figure out how to return two of them. So this commandment is as much a message to myself as it is to you. Before you check out, check out the return policy. A lot of places allow you to return items in store, which I know goes against the idea of shopping online in the first place, but it can end up being the easiest solution in the long run if you have an issue with an order. Also websites have varying restrictions and policies, so it can't hurt to keep yourself aware.

10. **Thou shalt covet thy neighbor's possessions:** Don't feel ashamed if you feel mega envious of someone's outfit on Instagram or someone's accessories on Snapchat. It's not jealousy, it's inspiration. Pinterest could be considered the most polite burn book of all time, but instead we consider it one big vision board. One of the biggest ways I learn about new online shops and trends is through social media. By watching "favorites" videos on YouTube or browsing Instagram's "explore" page, I learn about all different types of products and people and places. I don't like to call it "stalking," I like to call it "style studying."

CLEANING
OUT
YOUR CLOSET
FLOWCHART

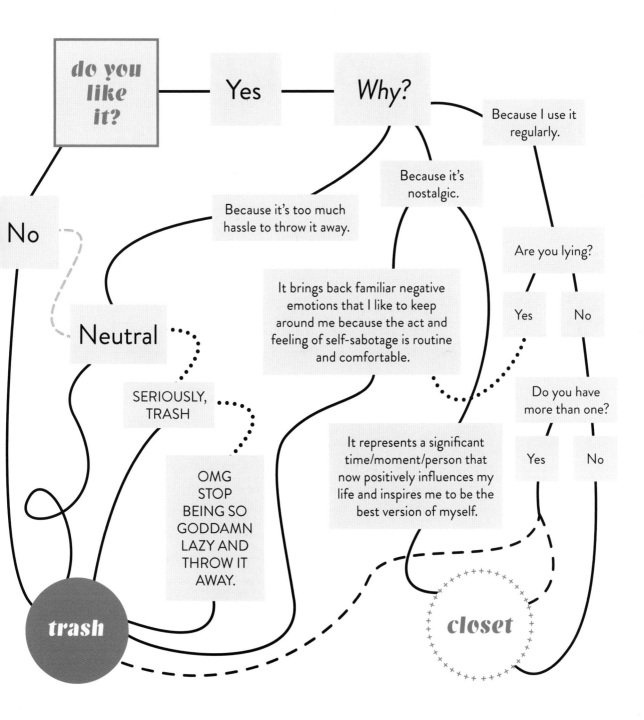

do you like it?

Yes ——— *Why?*

Because I use it regularly.

Because it's nostalgic.

No

Because it's too much hassle to throw it away.

Are you lying?

Neutral

It brings back familiar negative emotions that I like to keep around me because the act and feeling of self-sabotage is routine and comfortable.

Yes   No

SERIOUSLY, TRASH

Do you have more than one?

OMG STOP BEING SO GODDAMN LAZY AND THROW IT AWAY.

It represents a significant time/moment/person that now positively influences my life and inspires me to be the best version of myself.

Yes   No

trash

closet

the seven deadly sins

OF TRAVEL STYLE

Traveling is what separates the businessmen from the adult babies.

I've traveled a lot over the past ten years, and because of that I've developed my own sense of travel style. It's one part giving zero sh*ts and six parts sweatpants. The rules of fashion go out the window when you travel, so style is anyone's game. Through many of my own trials and tribulations, I've developed the Seven Deadly Sins of Travel Style. These are the sins we commonly commit when we get dressed to go.

Pride

Sometimes we let our vanity make our decisions and end up thinking we'll be *fine* traveling in our fancy clothes. Wrong. Travel is uncomfortable by default, so the least you can do is give yourself some breathable fabric and a fighting chance. Even if you have to

head directly to a formal event when you get out of your plane, train, or automobile, there are small things you can do to create a more comfortable scenario.

- Pack thick travel socks or slippers.
- Pack a "travel costume"—comfortable clothes you can change into mid-trip and change back out of just before you arrive.
- Make sure to bring the Travel Trinity: dry shampoo, deodorant, and toothpaste.

Envy

Before you walk out your door, schedule fifteen minutes to assess your gear. Do you have/need underwear, socks, a sweatshirt, a jacket, an umbrella, your passport? It's extra uncomfortable to toss and turn while trying to fall asleep only to look to your left and see a stranger *living* for their neck pillow. You know, that thing you forgot. Preparation is always in style.

Gluttony

I don't know about you, but when I travel I treat myself. I say I'll travel "healthy" and "wholesome," but when push comes to shove, I will push and shove people to get French fries on my layover. I make sure to pack clothes with a little extra give for my getaways. Why create extra reasons to feel self-conscious by packing only body-hugging options? There are plenty of fancy sweatpants in the world that can be accessorized into a stylish ensemble.

Lust

When I travel, my cash becomes Monopoly money to me. It doesn't seem real, so buying clothing I'm lusting after in foreign lands is fiiiiiiine. But be careful! Not only do you need the funds to back up your thread thirst, you need the space. At this point it's embarrassing the amount of times I've had to buy an extra bag when I'm away just so I can fit all the other stuff I bought without thinking. Don't always trust your lust.

Anger

At home I usually pack an assortment of mix-and-match options so my traveling self can create outfits when I get to my destination. I always think I'm doing myself a favor by allowing myself future fashion freedom. This way, I can see how I'm feeling when I get there and choose something suitable, rather than trying to predict what I'll feel best in. But that's not really why I use this method. The reality is that when I'm packing, I don't want to make any decisions, so I leave my wardrobe open-ended for my traveling self to figure out. But the problem with this is that my packing self and my traveling self are THE same SELF. Once I'm in my hotel, I still can't make decisions and hate everything I've packed. To avoid this I need to pack with more specific ensembles in mind. When I give myself too many wardrobe options, I also give myself the option to get angry. Which is not a good look. Neither is an existential crisis.

Greed

It's extremely easy to want to bring ALL THE OUTFITS with you when you travel. This is the sin I commit constantly. My brain assumes every possible scenario that could happen in the twenty-four hours I'm away and thinks that I should be prepared. Yes, of course I need two pairs of rain boots—what if I hate one when I get there? Three dresses and a couple of romper options for one night? OF course. I've gotten slightly better over the years, but it's still something I struggle with. Do as I write, not as I might. Try to pack only what you'll need, with one backup option if necessary.

Sloth

Don't wait until the last available minute to pack. We both know it's the worst. You'll end up at your destination with a single sock, twelve pairs of underwear, and the trench coat you got on sale three years ago but have never worn. Give yourself some time to develop your fashion strategy and then implement the appropriate packing.

Friday, Dec. 25, 2015

Dear Diary,

I can't believe I found you! I thought I had completely lost you in the chaos and confusion of Black Friday, but THANK GOD you're alive! I will say you've seen better days, no offense, Diary, but at least you're here! You can't tell, but I'm hugging you!

So let me fill you in on everything that's happened. The night before Black Friday, my G-Wind showed up out of nowhere! She came bursting through my door ready to rumble. When I asked her how she knew what was happening, since incoming and outgoing mail for freshmen is a complete disaster the first few months at the MOA, she told me that Dr. Scholls had been filling her in every step of the way. She said she never intended on forcing me into the MWOA, and really wanted me to know this wasn't a setup. I told her it was *kind of* a setup, but a setup of the best kind. She kept telling me how incredibly proud of me she was and how she's always known I had it in me to lead this revolution, but she wanted me to do it on my own. I told her it'd been a lot of hard work, a lot of tears, and, you guessed it, a lot of sweat. But it's been amazing. As I started to tell her about everything we've been doing and all the groups that we've been organizing, I felt myself swelling with all kinds of emotions until I finally collapsed on the ground, sobbing.

G-Wind ran to my side and wrapped her wrinkled arms around me. I didn't understand why I was so emotional. I hugged my G-Wind, sniffling and snuffling, until I suddenly let out the words "I'm just so happy." And that's exactly what it was. I finally felt happy. This uprising, though it was intended for the greater good, was lifting *me* up, it was giving *me* my purpose, and making *me* feel like I had value and that I belong. And that's exactly how I wanted other unwanted wares to feel. Like they had worth. It might seem like the button-up business shirts and six-inch stilettos run the world, but every single one of us has potential and has importance. We all have a purpose.

As soon as I finished my cheesy spiel, I looked up and saw Birk, Rees, and Dr. Scholls standing in my doorway. I immediately felt embarrassed, but the three of them, along with G-Wind, started clapping until Birk finally said, "Are you ready, SOTI? It's just about time." I nodded and we all headed out of my storage unit and back to the BFF.

On the way out I could hear Dr. Scholls say, "Hey, Wind, it's good to see you. You look great."

"You *heeled* pretty nicely yourself," my G-Wind replied. OOF, that's where I get it from, Diary!

We got to the BFF and it was a frenzy of excitement and anticipation. Dr. Scholls made his way through the commotion of clothing to the mic at the podium—or rather a busted karaoke machine on top of a couple of old Payless bogo shoe boxes. I could hear the start of murmurs in the crowd: "Is that her?" "OMG, I think that's her." It sounded like different items had started recognizing G-Wind.

Dr. Scholls spoke softly into the mic. "Everyone, please settle down." The crowd wasn't listening. "Please, apparel, I need you to quiet down." Still no change.

Finally my G-Wind grabbed the mic. "LISTEN UP, FASHION FREAKS. STITCH IT OR BITCH IT. AND IF YOU'RE GONNA BITCH IT, THEN YOU BETTER EXIT." The room was immediately silent, in pure awe of my G-Wind. I couldn't help but grin like an idiot.

"Thank you, Wind," Dr. Scholls said, gently taking back the microphone and continuing. "My fellow surplus. No matter what happens, today we are inspiring change. The Brooks Brothers, as many of you know them, have become the Crooks Brothers," he said. "They've stolen the value from each one of us and they continue to invest it in 'more *desirable* designer wear.' Well, not anymore. Today we take a stand. Today we reevaluate our value. Today we show them that we have more to offer than the price at which they offer us!" The room was riled up and Dr. Scholls was practically yelling like I've never heard before. "They can mark down our cost, but they can never take away our inherent worth!" He slammed the mic down and the room erupted with cheers and applause.

Wow.

I looked at G-Wind, who was applauding with a look of adoration. It gave me a clear glimpse into the social-justice-based romance they must have had, like, back in their heyday. G-Wind caught my eye and shook herself out of her love fog, shrugging her shoulders at me like she couldn't believe Dr. Scholls had it in him.

Just then Rees leaned into me and whispered, "I feel like I just watched a scene from *Braveheart*." I looked at him, confused; he clinked a buckle at me and smiled. I nearly pissed my pants right there, Diary! But instead I contained myself as much as I could and smiled back.

Dr. Scholls then introduced my G-Wind, who at that point needed no introduction. "Let me introduce you to an old friend of mine," he started. A smattering of "oohs" and "ahhs" came from the crowd, because even though we considered ourselves intelligent progressives, we were still a bunch of immature high schoolers. "Okay, settle down," he went on. "I'm sure many of you know who she is. But you might not know that Wind is the reason we're all here in this room today. It was her unyielding desire for outfit equality years ago and her passion for pricing impartiality that founded the MWOA. Unfortunately, her fight for fairness forced her to surrender her student status."

Again, G-Wind grabbed the mic. "But I'm back, motherfabrics! Let's show these Brooks Brothers what a real family can do!" G-Wind pointed directly at me. "Let's sweat the mall stuff!" The crowd went COMPLETELY nuts!

Suddenly Birk ran to the podium holding up an old iPhone 5. "You guys, YOU GUYS! Look! It's happening!" She held the iPhone to the microphone so we could hear the video that was playing. It was a YouTube video called "Black FriSLAY" and it had been posted twenty minutes earlier by Tyler Oakley.

"Hi, everybody, my name's Tyler Oakley and welcome to another edition of *Q and Slay*." He began clapping along with an unheard beat. "Rosie on Twitter asks Tyler how's your Christmas shopping going? Well, Rosie, let me tell you that my Christmas shopping just got a whole lot merrier because my favorite shopping holiday is back. And we all know I like my shopping holidays like I like my coffee—cheap and black. That's right, y'all, Black Friday is back!"

OMG. Tyler Oakley just told the world that Black Friday is back. We all looked at each other, silent and stunned. Until G-Wind got on the mic and yelled, "God bless that beautiful twink! You heard 'em, y'all! Black Friday is back!" The room erupted into controlled chaos. Everyone knew their job and everyone was going to work. We were a well-oiled machine.

Walkers got into their formations, led by Rees (swoon!), and headed out into the mall, posting signs exactly as planned. Stalkers, organized by Dr. Scholls and with their backup signage in tow, manned their battle stations. Our talkers were already all over social media. Birk was at the helm making sure we were blasting Tyler's video everywhere and alerting any contacts we had at local radio stations and local publications. "Hannah Hart just reblogged Tyler's video on Tumblr," one of our talkers yelled from the back, and the room cheered.

Black Friday was really happening.

We had one hour until the MOA was set to open and everything was in motion. G-Wind and I had maintained our postings at the BFF vision board, communicating with the heads of each assembly, overseeing all of the activity, and making sure we were on target. The time flew by, and before we knew it, most of our signs and stalkers were stationed and there was only fifteen minutes left until doors opened.

"Brooks Brothers have been spotted in Brookstone!" yelled a misshapen Forever 21 sports bra from her talker station.

"Shit!" I responded without thinking. But my G-Wind didn't seem to catch it. "The Brooks Brothers aren't supposed to get out of their mahogany chest for at least another hour!"

We had been monitoring the Brothers' schedule for weeks. Every morning they arose from their classic mahogany chest at seven on the dot to start their predictable schedule of starch, polish, repeat. Luckily a lot of the MOA security members had recently become MWOA members, so the plan had been to set up our sales overnight and have the doors unlocked at 6 a.m. before the Brooks Brothers even had a chance to button up. But it was now 5:50 a.m. and the Brooks Brothers were already up and about. This was a Code Red!

"Where's Scholls?" G-Wind asked.

Scholls's voice came in over a walkie. "I'm being prodded by some Prada at the moment. I'm out of stock at the moment!"

"Shit!" my G-Wind responded without thinking.

I jumped in. "Rees, what's your status?"

Rees responded with a broken connection. "Sweat, I'm…stuck…not…lucky."

"His coordinates say he's in the Lucky Denim store," Birk chimed in.

"They must have trapped him in it," I said.

"Brooks Brothers are said to be on the move toward Nordstrom," said the F21 sports bra.

"Oh, yeah?" G-Wind said. "Well then, let's party." G-Wind started to make her way out of the room.

"G-Wind, where are you going?" I shouted, but she didn't respond. "G-Wind! I'm coming with you!" I raced after my G-Wind and out the door. Her old MWOA legs kicked right back in because she was a goddang speed demon. I could barely keep up with her.

We raced through crowds of confused clothing and clearance signs. More and more students were starting to wake up. I looked up at the giant clock in the food court: it read 5:55 a.m. We weaved through the wardrobe and made our way to Nordstrom. "What are we going to do?" I asked G-Wind.

"Just stay close," she responded. She rushed through the entrance and headed straight for the shoe department. In the middle of the department was Dr. Scholls, strung up by his heels with an old pair of shoelaces, surrounded by Prada pumps.

"Dr. Scholls!" I screamed.

"I'm okay, I'm okay," he choked out.

"Well, well, well, there she is. That cheap pile of polyester I thought we got rid of years ago." We turned and saw the Brooks Brothers standing by the register.

"Hey, fellas! Well, would you look at that? You know, I doubted it, but it's nice to see you two assholes finally found a girlfriend," G-Wind replied, gesturing to the cash register. I couldn't help but giggle.

"We knew you'd be back," they sneered.

"Did you now?" G-Wind said.

"Of course we did! Because you're a bargain-basement-rack basic."

"Take that back!" I yelled.

G-wind placed a hand on my shoulder and said, "Just let them finish, Sweat."

"That's right. You're a wannabe, Wind. Look at you: your colors are faded, your design is outdated, and worst of all, you're completely synthetic." The Brothers continued to vomit their gross, elitist nonsense and I couldn't understand why G-Wind was just taking it. Until I spotted Birk in the corner of the store with a security guard. She pointed at the clock, which read 5:58 a.m. G-Wind knew exactly what she was doing.

"Don't forget the annoying noise I make when I walk," G-Wind said.

"Yeah! When you walk it sounds like a garbage bag falling down a trash chute. How appropriate." The Brothers got closer to G-Wind. "The MOA gave you a chance to better yourself, to evolve yourself into something worthwhile. You could have been just like a velour Juicy Couture jumpsuit or a high-end Puma track jacket. But you took the opportunity that was given to you and you wasted it. Why? Because *you're waste*. You're a low-cost, commercial garbage bag, and that's all you'll ever be," they hissed.

"You're right," G-Wind replied. "I do come at a low cost. But I've got high value. And somewhere in that high-quality cotton and overcompensation, you have value, too."

"Yeah, we start at one hundred and twenty dollars," said one of the Brothers.

"Not today," G-Wind replied, sticking a 60 percent clearance sticker on each of them. "It's Black Friday, gentlemen! Let's party!"

G-Wind whistled and the doors burst open! Crowds of bargain hunters began to flood the MOA. It was a beautiful pandemonium of price cuts.

Everything happened so fast it was hard to keep track of what happened until the dust settled. And I know you won't believe the outcome, but just trust me, it's all true.

My G-Wind got scooped up by a redheaded Southern firecracker named Mamrie Hart, who kept muttering to her tiny hairless dog with its tongue hanging all over the place that it'd be great to use in a video. She also ended up grabbing Dr. Scholls after her friend joked with her about fixing her foot odor. That friend was Hannah Hart, who wound up purchasing Birk after she won a game of rock-paper-scissors with their third friend, who also wanted Birk—Grace Helbig. But it's okay that she didn't get Birk (no offense, Birk!) because Grace purchased something almost as cool...me!

Black Friday was a complete success. And as G-Wind, Dr. Scholls, Birk, and I started to leave with our new owners, I couldn't help but feel a sense of sadness that something was missing. But just then Mamrie said, "Grace, these are so you." I looked up and saw that she was holding Rees!

"Yup. Done," Grace said, and quickly made the purchase, tossing Rees into the bag with me.

"I think this worked out pretty good, *overall*. Don't you?" Rees said. I stared at him until he finally said, "That sounded real dumb, right?"

"Big-time."

"I know. I'm new at this."

"Don't worry, I'll help you."

"I guess I should probably buckle up, then, huh?"

"Okay, stop this." Rees and I joked all the way to our new home.

Rumor has it that the Brooks Brothers were bought by some nerdy MIT botany grad student named Tim who wore them to a job interview once, then lost them to the gross shadows of his closet in his Boston apartment.

I guess you could say the outcome of Black Friday was wonderfully fitting.

Sorry, Diary!

Sincerely,
Sweatpants

last looks

Sometimes you wake up and you just don't want to face your face. Or your hair. Or your body. Or your closet. Or the day. Sometimes you wake up and you just don't feel pretty. And it feels petty even wishing you felt pretty, but you can't deny that you're distracted by your own depressing mind-set.

And in those moments of repetitive, negative thoughts, it's almost impossible to allow yourself to feel good (trust me, I know). But if you have one ounce of try in you, I ask you to try saying one or some of these mantras to yourself and see if it makes a difference. If it doesn't, congrats, you're still depressed, how much familiar fun are we having? If it does make a difference, congrats! Breaking cycles is as difficult as trying to break a bicycle with your bare hands! You're doing it!

ELEVENTH-HOUR INSPIRATIONS:

1. I'm not the worst! Yes, I'm talking to myself out loud and alone, but I'm not the worst!

2. Today doesn't have to be the best. But as long as I don't sh*t in my pants in the pantry section of a Target, everything will be okay.

3. Even Beyoncé gets bloated.

4. Judge my body all you want, society, but what you don't know is that inside this body that you deem unattractive is a brain thinking about a bunch of happy puppies rolling down a hill. Just try to judge that.

5. I'm good enough, I'm smart enough, and daggone it, we're all going to be dirt in the ground, so who cares how many likes I get on my Instagram photo.

6. Compassion is high fashion.

7. Good intentions are great accessories.

8. Today, my purse will be my only baggage.

9. Today, I will be like my face powder: even, available, and translucent.

10. Fashions fade, but dumb is forever.

Congratulations! You made it through this fun thought-swamp of senselessness! Are you the better for it? I can't say. But I can say thank you for activating your curiosity and for reading this book.

Beauty and style, though at one point destructive and difficult topics for me to reflect on in isolation, have now become fascinating and funny things for me to think about openly.

In the past few decades I've learned that it's wildly unfulfilling to measure someone's worth by looking at them. But it's ridiculously exciting to discover someone's self by soaking in their perspective.

Don't get me wrong, bodies are beautiful and confidence is striking, but balance is key. If you're ever feeling physically inadequate, remember that at the end of the day we're all just a herd of human sock puppets. If every single human being on this earth were a "perfect" specimen of "beauty" as defined by current magazines and fashion shows, this would be THE DUMBEST PLANET EVER. Please, I BEG you, take a second and really try to imagine EVERY SINGLE HUMAN ON EARTH as a Victoria's Secret model. Babies to men in their eighties. ALL VICTORIA'S SECRET MODELS. Your father-in-law, Victoria's Secret model.

Bodies are beautiful and stupid. Surround yourself with souls that inspire you.

They say beauty is only skin-deep. But over time skin sags. And SAG is an organization for professional actors. Therefore, beauty is all an act. And let's be real, none of us are getting Oscars.

I know what you're thinking. You think I forgot about the five tips for preventing camel toe that I promised you in the introduction of this book. WELL I DIDN'T FORGET. So you can delete your scathing Amazon review right now because here are . . .

FIVE WAYS
TO AVOID
CAMEL TOE

1. Panty liners. I've worn a surprising number of spandex suits over the last two years. Like, more than three. More than enough to know that they show *everything*. Trust me, you don't know how stupid your body can be until you jam it into some spandex and see what tries to escape. Invest in some panty liners; they make molehills out of mountains.

2. Low riders. Only wear clothing with low crotches.

3. Wear a wooden barrel as clothing like an old-timey town drunk.

4. Look into medical operations to smooth over your crotch region like a Barbie Doll.

5. Use a time machine to prevent camels from getting on Noah's ark.

thank you to...

...my editor, Lauren Spiegel, who has an incredible soul and coped with my months of writer's block by doing the only thing I would understand: getting a dog. Also by being a wonderfully patient, nurturing, and collaborative human being.

...my photographer, Robin Roemer, for blindly accepting and completely dominating the challenge of photographing a book that wasn't written yet. You're an amazing talent who's too humble for your own dumb brilliance!

...my amazingly talented designer, Shawn Dahl, who has elevated this book (and my first book) to levels of charming and delightful adorableness that I could have only ever imagined ogling on Pinterest.

...my assistant and the major reason I operate anywhere close to "normal" on a daily basis, Diane Kang. God bless your young, high-functioning brain and affinity for snacks.

...my parents for always wondering where I am and if I'm okay. And for being so supportive and excited about the things I'm doing that don't make sense.

...my mom for, again, sprinkling her personal words of wisdom throughout this book and for unknowingly allowing me to compare her makeup-selling days to drug trafficking.

...my 100 percent for being you.

...my professional team, Ken and Erin, for all the supportive (Erin) and distracting (Ken) emails.

...YOU who reads this book and watches my videos and supported any of my previous endeavors. YOU f*cking rule it—and I can't thank YOU enough for taking any of YOUR time to pay attention to my dumb. Thank you.

...YOU who reads this book and doesn't know me—thank you for listening. It's a very rare thing to experience with strangers, so truly, thank you.

...any dogs that have evolved with the ability to read, thanks for choosing my book to test out your cool new brains.

DON'T MISS

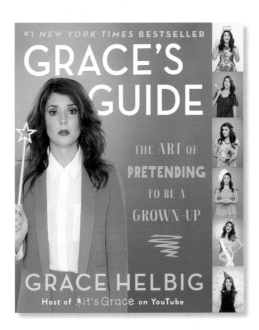

"Grace Helbig is my spirit animal."

—Jenny Han, author of *To All the Boys I've Loved Before*